THE TRANSFORMATIVE MIND AND SOUL

HOW TO USE NLP TO IMPROVE INDIVIDUAL AND ORGANISATIONAL PERFORMANCE?

DR. AMIT DAS

Copyright © Dr. Amit Das
All Rights Reserved.

This book has been published with all efforts taken to make the material error-free after the consent of the author. However, the author and the publisher do not assume and hereby disclaim any liability to any party for any loss, damage, or disruption caused by errors or omissions, whether such errors or omissions result from negligence, accident, or any other cause.

While every effort has been made to avoid any mistake or omission, this publication is being sold on the condition and understanding that neither the author nor the publishers or printers would be liable in any manner to any person by reason of any mistake or omission in this publication or for any action taken or omitted to be taken or advice rendered or accepted on the basis of this work. For any defect in printing or binding the publishers will be liable only to replace the defective copy by another copy of this work then available.

To

All my bosses and students who made a difference in my professional career.

"A thoughtful inquiry has the power to drastically shift someone's perspective and alter their course of action. For instance, ask yourself this question often: What is the best question to ask right now? The best way to discover your potential is to act as though you can do it. I presume you can. You won't do what you are unable to do. You will learn whether it is indeed impossible, so don't worry. And make sure to implement the essential safety precautions if necessary. You won't ever know if something is feasible or not as long as you think it is impossible."

- Dr. Amit Das, Motivational Speaker, Leadership Coach and Mentor.

Contents

Foreword — *vii*

Preface — *xv*

Acknowledgements — *xxiii*

1. Fundamentals Of Nlp — 1

2. Build Self-confidence And Boost Your Performance — 20

3. Facilitating Learning Intelligence Through Nlp — 40

4. Transforming Organisation Through Nlp — 72

References — 89

About The Author — 93

Foreword

Dear Reader,

Thank you for taking the time to learn more about "The Transformative Mind & Soul" to get the life what you want. These days, NLP teaches its adherents how to develop these potent talents, which mirror those of some of the most successful individuals in the world. This book is the first of a series of brief, easy-to-read publications for individuals who wish to take advantage of this system of human transformation but don't have the time to fully understand the enormous depth of theories and methods that this area has to offer.

Are you interested in NLP? Do you want to discover how it may benefit you?

This book takes you on a journey that emphasises how you may apply NLP in personal development, communication, business, health, and other areas of life while providing answers to the most frequently asked questions we hear about NLP.

Have you ever read something that truly moved you? Where in your life would you most like to experience this sense of inspiration?

Each of us is born with a brain that functions as an internal supercomputer. However, others claim that humans are only able to access a small portion of its potential. Many people discover that using effective NLP techniques makes it simple to attract more success and fulfilment into their lives. Change your mind right now and realise your full potential! This book will teach you to accept the fact that you are distinct from every other person you meet. You are all unique, whether you are at work, home, or meeting up with friends. Everyone has a different outlook on life, which is influenced by their experiences, upbringing, surroundings, interactions, and a variety of other things. These distinctions are not unfavourable.

What will you learn from this book?

NLP establishes liberating perspectives and assumptions about people, communication, and what change entails while providing each person with the skills and resources necessary to build their own condition of perfection. You'll learn how your behaviours are closely related to your internal dialogue in the pages of this book and how to alter it to enhance every part of your life. Additionally, you'll see how being sympathetic and empathic towards other people will improve your communication skills and encourage others to lean on you for assistance.

You'll discover how speaking to individuals in their native language and going for a walk may both help you resolve conflicts. Additionally, you'll learn how to use the success factors in combination with the power of your imagination to easily accomplish both short-term and long-term goals. Additionally, you'll study mental states and how they affect our capacity for critical thought and sense of self. When you begin to use neuro-linguistic programming in ways you never imagined, the world will become more accessible to you.

This book has all the information you need to get started using NLP to capture empowering states and programme more of them into your future so you can achieve your own state of greatness. Even if you are unfamiliar with NLP, if you are truly ready to change now and are not scared to step outside of your comfort zone, then yes, this book is for you! This book gives you a basic knowledge of and grasp of the essential principles, along with useful and thought-provoking tasks. It also exposes you to the primary topics and ideas of NLP.

This book also discusses individuals' reading habits and how to easily persuade others to have an impact on their lives. The reality is that everyone has the power to influence another person, and while most choose not to take advantage of others, there are certain sinister souls who relish doing so. This book details the exact steps involved in using and implementing each mind control method.

Are you even aware that you have the power to change any unfavourable thoughts you are having into ones that aren't? And even better, banish any negative ideas that come to mind. Whatever your thoughts may be, there is a way to alter them for the better. You'll have an edge by analysing individuals in social, professional, and personal settings. Although most of us subconsciously analyse one another, very few people control this talent and master it. Therefore, doing so will provide you with advantages that others are losing out on. This book is for people who wish to live a happier, healthier, and more prosperous life, or in one word, success, because NLP also eliminates any limiting beliefs you may have.

This book offers a personal and interpersonal programme that allows you to improve your ability to control your emotions rather than letting them rule you, to manage your motivations, to be less judgmental, to be more productive, to be more assured, to be more adaptable, to be more persuasive, to be liked and respected. Enhancing creativity, collaboration, cooperation, and communication are the topics covered.

Why is your subconscious mind the most significant factor in determining how you feel?

NLP is used by every successful person, some of whom are unaware of it. In today's environment, success is achieved by those who can manage their emotions for the good of their lives. The answer to your question, "How can I possibly retain positivity throughout my entire life?" is that you can't. However, you may change your perspective such that you stop having negative thoughts or that they are replaced with positive ones.

NLP may help you become a better leader, build stronger bonds with others, be a better parent and friend, and even work with people as a coach or therapist. Actually, everything in your life needs to be improved You may quickly learn the skills provided by NLP to make significant changes in your life. Millions of individuals have already benefited from NLP by overcoming phobias, boosting confidence, enhancing relationships, and achieving better success.

Can you recall a time when you were in the great outdoors, surrounded by various tones of green and quiet sounds? Where in your life would it be helpful to be able to achieve this condition of serenity and peace?

This book's professional research can guarantee that you'll gain improved communication skills, the ability to programme your own brain, and the capacity to discern someone's thoughts and feelings right away—even if you're socially awkward and have no knowledge of the human mind at all. Therefore, you should read this book if you want to develop your talents as a master of human analysis and learn from the best people in the world.

Finding one's true self, identity, and purpose is at the heart of NLP. It offers a framework for comprehending and connecting to the physical side of human experiences, which extend beyond the individual and into family, community, and global systems. NLP encompasses wisdom and vision in addition to expertise and performance. Most people will, at some point in their lives, feel the most confident they have ever been, even if it was years ago and may have only lasted for a few seconds. The benefit of NLP is that it enables the user to tap into this resource and expand upon that confident state. This is probably already familiar to you, but I'll go over more specifics and tips for gaining access to these states.

This book is particularly developed for those learning NLP for the first time. It provides clear explanations of fundamental ideas and gives step-by-step methods for resolving a range of issues. You'll learn how to alter the attitudes and convictions that hold you back from success, as well as the long-kept trick to wise life planning. The book "The Transformative Mind & Soul" is an easy-to-understand introduction to neuro-linguistic programming that covers all the essential information in only seven condensed chapters. You'll learn how to improve your communication skills and build stronger relationships with people. You'll also learn how to modify the things in your life that aren't working and boost the things that are.

Some people seem to have more talent than others. One of the most rapidly expanding areas of applied psychology, NLP, explains in plain words what they do differently and makes it possible for you to pick up these patterns of greatness. You will learn how to guide others in the direction of your choice by mimicking their behaviour in order to influence them towards a desired end. This book will act as a guide, written in straightforward language, to help you motivate others to accomplish what you want them to do gladly.

Do you ever wish you could rewire yourself so you could communicate effectively and win someone over right away?

Leading life coach, mentor, presenter, and counsellor Dr. Amit Das reveals in this book how our mental health affects every action we do. Because changing your thoughts may transform your life, he offers ways of implementing minor internal adjustments that will have a significant external impact.

Then you should continue reading. You will discover the following things inside this book:

- Recognising and utilising body language.
- How to approach and attain the desired goals.
- Getting rid of stress and negative emotions.
- Overcome phobias, anxieties, and frustrations.
- Quickly modify even ingrained behaviours.
- Managing and recovering from trauma and phobia.
- Heal emotional wounds from the past.
- Successful negotiations, sales, and meetings techniques for accelerated learning.
- Quickly and effortlessly alter your emotional state.
- Reset your internal programming to alter your future.

This book will help you on your path to self-mastery by providing step-by-step exercises for each method. So stop searching if you're seeking for the book to help you succeed in life. The one for you is this. Pick up this book right away. The author of this book has compiled information from the murkiest studies of brain science and the most effective NLP techniques. Before being informed of the enormous levels of controversy that NLP has over the long run, you will first be shown exactly what it is.

What do you wish you could "do better"?

This book serves as an introduction to the fundamental principles of NLP for those who are just starting to learn more about it. These principles cover thoughts, emotions, behaviours, awareness, linguistics, the nervous system, general semantics, rep systems, and submodalities, among many other important topics. This book will provide you with the foundations you need to properly learn the fundamentals of NLP in an approachable manner, with straightforward explanations and no "fluff." Uses for this Information What value is your understanding of people analysis if you don't know how to put it to use? This book will not only teach you how to interpret body language and personality indicators, but it will also provide you with practical advice on how to use it. You may alter your own state of mind by altering your body language, as you will discover in this book.

The book gives you all the knowledge you need to make the most of your training and to do the following things: feel more assured in your ability to launch and manage a successful business; deliver effective therapy and coaching sessions; assist your clients in overcoming problems such as anxiety, insomnia, phobias, obesity, confidence issues, and others; and much more. All levels of NLP interest and expertise should read this, and it's a terrific tool for anybody who wants to become a good coach, therapist, or counsellor. In the end, NLP serves as a tool to research greatness. How do successful people and organisations get where they are? People think that we may start looking at that illusive structure by employing all the aforementioned components of Neuro Linguistic Programming, which is the technique used by NLP to locate the solution. Such a desired result is undoubtedly abstract.

However, dismantling the framework of subjective experience would also require learning how to free individuals from their painful, constrained, and tiny viewpoints that keep them bound to dysfunctional routines. In essence, NLP helps us humans achieve what we want to do more effectively. The application of NLP will quickly improve many aspects of your life. Get a decent NLP book, then just follow the directions! Thank you in anticipation for taking the time to read this book.

So, happy reading and learning to all my readers.

Carpe diem.

Dr. Amit Das

Motivational Speaker, Leadership Coach, and Mentor.

Preface

"The truth is, people don't stay the same. People either get better or they get worse."
— Richard Bandler

Whether you are pursuing personal or professional development, neurolinguistic programming is a crucial component of growth and development. By being open to new ways of acting, thinking, and seeing, you may improve your life, your experiences, and your perceptions. Neuro-linguistic programming makes this possible.

Since a few years ago, the three letters "NLP" have become more frequent in this context. NLP, however, has a strong relationship with selective perception as well as communication. However, what precisely is its purpose and how can business owners, salesmen, students, and workers profit from it? The techniques and potential of neurolinguistic programming (NLP) are crucial.

Starting with the past, it was created in the 1970s by John Grinder and Richard Bandler. Typically, it is founded on a series of ideas, declarations, or actions. It claims to be founded on pseudoscience, which indicates that it is only partially based on science. It is a paradigm focused on communication. The meaning of the name is given below.

Neuro: Neuro has to do with the mind or the brain. How a person's conduct and mental condition impact communication That is why the word "neuro" is used.

Linguistic: It is associated with language, as the term suggests. Language is the fundamental form of communication, as is common knowledge. Communication is constantly governed by language differences. The majority of information is sent by mouth, or verbal communication, and body language.

Programing: According to this philosophy, three key actions must be taken in order to succeed. First, a person must know how to accomplish something in order to succeed. Repeating a procedure indicates that there should be consistency in it. Success comes from being consistent. If you want a different outcome, alter the procedure.

A mental process called neuro-etymological programming (NLP) involves studying the strategies used by successful individuals and using them to achieve a personal goal. NLP is one of the most astounding and fundamental human abilities, along with brain research. Over time, NLP techniques have gained popularity as a sort of therapy that many individuals are choosing to employ. This type of programming has been repeatedly shown to be a very successful form of treatment when people are trying to accomplish particular goals and get rid of certain concerns. This book discusses what neuro-linguistic programming is and the many advantages of utilising it. NLP investigates the connections between our language, neuronal, and behavioural patterns as well as our emotional states (programmes). According to the theory, people can adopt more effective methods of thinking, speaking, feeling, and behaving by studying NLP, according to the theory.

How did you feel when you considered achieving this objective in the past? What did you do, not do, or fail to do in order to accomplish that goal?

Think back for a minute to a period when you were attempting to accomplish a goal, such as losing a few pounds, finding happiness, improving your relationship, getting a better career, etc. Now consider the accomplishment or failure of that aim. Did you succeed or fail in achieving your objective, for instance, if it was to land a better job? It is quite useful to use neurolinguistic programming. It makes it possible for you to think and act with greater effectiveness. NLP teaches you how to master your mind, which has a significant impact on how you conduct your life. Additionally, it includes a collection of methods you may use to apply NLP and adjust whatever you want.

An overview of one of the most potent psychological strategies now available and how you might use it to improve your life. You are who you are because of your differences. Start becoming familiar with NLP techniques right away! You will benefit from participating in various situations and see an improvement in your relationships and interactions with your audiences. You could find the solutions you're looking for in this book. In NLP, success is used as a mental model to achieve the desired result. You may use the methods you learn in this book to achieve your objectives and improve your self-awareness in everyday situations.

Have you ever wondered how one approach could help you improve your self-esteem, understand people, overcome phobias and anxieties, improve your communication skills, learn how to resolve disagreements peacefully, and set and achieve goals?

By developing your mind-body connection and understanding NLP techniques, you can master your life. Your success in both your personal and professional life can be accelerated by it. The techniques of NLP are used by top achievers in every area of life. You will learn everything you need to know about NLP from this insightful book, enabling you to fulfil your personal objectives. With the help of this fast-start NLP book, you will discover the precise steps to using the art of NLP and improving your life as well as the lives of others!

You may benefit yourself with NLP while simultaneously assisting others. When you feel better about yourself, you carry yourself more confidently and inspire others to do the same. As you share neuro-linguistic programming with others, you will acquire the vocabulary you need to connect with others on a true level and discover methods to uplift them. You'll discover that you're developing more solid bonds with others, making stronger connections at work, and raising kids who are more certain and competent.

Are you sick of having the same bad habits yet unsure of how to alter them?

If you said "yes" to any of them, neuro-linguistic programming may be the solution you've been looking for to make a big difference in your life. You may become a powerful, joyful, successful person and realise your goals by utilising the straightforward NLP procedures. In NLP, success is used as a mental model to achieve the desired result. You may use the methods you learn in this book to reach your objectives and improve your self-awareness in everyday situations.

Utilise NLP to achieve amazing personal achievements right away. Do you wish to interact with others in a more secure manner? Don't you still want to drift through life, to let everything pass you by? Would you wish to learn NLP to further your professional success? Communication is essential to society. It will enable you to exert more social influence and better comprehend the dialect of your own thoughts. But there are numerous ways to communicate incorrectly. The results of this poor communication include misunderstandings, disagreements, and a lack of progress.

Imagine for a moment that there is a tried-and-true technique that you can use to successfully influence others, get rid of all of your bad habits and thinking patterns, destroy your limiting beliefs, achieve more success than you ever thought possible, and create any desired desired result.

Wouldn't it be wonderful if there was a straightforward procedure that could aid in the analysis of your subconscious programming, the organisation of your current behavioural patterns, and the activation of your imagination to generate beneficial results? This is the connection between a person's thoughts and actions. NLP assists a worker in decision-making, knowledge and skill acquisition, and achieving desired outcomes. It is critical for both the individual and the company. Employees that speak the same language will be able to converse and comprehend each other better. A worker needs to listen more attentively in order to communicate more effectively. Language commonality facilitates greater communication in this way.

You'll see the advantages as soon as you include NLP into your daily practise. You have made a decision to go on the road to a happier, calmer, and more productive living by selecting NLP, which is a system that can actually change your life. Individuals can be evaluated by observing their body language and nonverbal cues. How to incorporate NLP into your social, professional, and personal life. Personal space parameters and their true meanings. A done-for-you exercise work guide to help you achieve the success and positivity you've been seeking. You may positively impact the people and circumstances around you by using NLP to make you feel good and appreciate who you are. NLP helps you learn how to filter information and get a more insightful understanding of a problem in their language. They will develop greater language skills when they discover that another person shares their opinion. Verbal communication accounts for 20% to 30% of communication, with tone of voice, pitch, body language, and posture also contributing.

In this book, four chapters are present. The first provides an overview of life coaching and NLP modelling from the past, emerging need of NLP while also examining new uses since Neuro-Linguistic Programming was originally created. In order to change, the greatest place to start is by knowing how our brains are built; thus, in this section, I'll look at the NLP fundamentals that will demonstrate how this is done. Then, you may do a few activities that show you how to alter your thinking so that you can accomplish your professional objectives, have a more optimistic outlook at work, and enhance your personal connections at work. This book aims to help readers better understand the various rules (or Meta-Programs) that regulate neurological and physiological interactions and the impact that these interactions and impacts have on our thoughts, feelings, and behaviours. This will help readers learn how to make conscious decisions that will promote the positive and healthy aspects of these interactions and impacts.

Building a purposeful life, buidling confidence to change your performance, and increasing focus at work with NLP and other techniques are provided in the second chapter. Apply the concepts in this book's ideas and techniques to your own life before moving on to others'. Your attitude, aptitude, and capacity for influencing and connecting with others will all quickly change.

The third section contains facilitating learning intelligence through NLP, fundamentals of mind control, manipulation, and understanding body language. These tools can be used as action plans for your coaching sessions.

The fourth or final section contains the role of the learning officer and HR Manager in using NLP and instructions on how to apply them to assist people in changing their behaviour and finding workplace satisfaction through neurolinguistic programming. This is the book to read if you want to learn the subtleties of using mind control and nerve pathways to accomplish your ultimate objective of success in life. Learn how to relate to others, comprehend what they are thinking, and influence them by using "mind reading" techniques, nonverbal communication, and "hearing what's missing." This book serves as a manual for professionals who want to excel at NLP and life coaching, complete with illustrations, forms, and comprehensive descriptions of the many techniques they can utilise. This is a brand-new, all-inclusive, mind-blowing guide to neurolinguistic programming is the new blueprint for your own ultimate achievement.

Those who coach using brain-based techniques are aware of the things that are most likely to alter your brain and will make particular suggestions to you. So how can you use this knowledge in your work? When a situation at work is challenging and you can't alter it, remind yourself or your team that you can still change your thinking. This will enable you to address problems more skillfully. No matter how old or set in your habits you are, your brain is always capable of positive change. Because of this, having neuroplasticity—the capacity to modify your brain—will enable you to operate more effectively. The exact brain adjustments you need to make will be a lot easier once you realise this is feasible. NLP enables you to stop any negative ideas we have about our coworkers in their tracks, which enhances our interactions with them. It is pointless to try to control people around us. Finding their shortcomings in ourselves and fixing them is a great strategy for isolating ourselves from the criticism we have about our coworkers. Most of the time, this prevents us from criticising and increases our tolerance and empathy.

"The most successful businesses have understood that their people are their fundamental competitive edge. Strategic business partners increasingly place more emphasis on human resources. Knowledge workers of today are referred to as knowledge workers. The study of data science and analytics has made information more accessible than ever. For human resource professionals, managing them, hiring them, and developing their skills is a significant task."- Dr. Amit Das

Acknowledgements

At the outset, I will thank my family for supporting me throughout the journey of writing my book and encouraging me to live my dreams; my son has always been instrumental in giving his inspiration to complete the writing of this book. Despite the fact that I am listed as the author of this book, "The Transformative Mind & Soul" would not have been published if I had depended entirely on my own talents. Creating this book required more than anything—it took a family of dedicated and caring people who were always prepared to lend a hand.

Writing a book while working full-time is no simple task, so I'd want to express my gratitude to my amazing coworkers who act as cheerleaders in equal measure. Thank you, too, to my students and clients for your patience and unflinching support while I worked on this book!

Thank you to everyone who has listened to me argue for doing everything you can to make your life, including your work life, more progressive. I appreciate everyone's assistance throughout the process. This book would not have been possible without each of you having had an impact on my life in some manner.

Lastly, I would like to thank all the people with whom I have been associated. You gave me power. I would like to thank Notion Press for publishing my book. Finally, thank you all for gifting your time to read this book.

I'd want to convey my heartfelt appreciation to the almighty God for bestowing his blessings and being so gracious.

CHAPTER ONE

Fundamentals Of NLP

"NLP provides us the ability to reject the preprogrammed ideas that have the potential to rule our present and future. We have the ability to alter these internal settings and hence change our lives. " -Tony Robbins

How might NLP help us reclaim control?

When it comes to studying NLP, the methods are a little different and heavily concentrated on utilising neurological processes (neuro), language (linguistic), and behavioural patterns hypothesised to attain certain life goals within a set amount of time. This study shows how NLP may be used in a variety of crucial fields, such as commerce, education, creative writing, health, family therapy, and interpersonal negotiation. The book, which is made up of a number of distinct pieces, serves as a practical manual for using NLP knowledge and methods in a variety of situations. Its goal is to demonstrate NLP's adaptability and aid managers, salesmen, instructors, psychologists, and parents in better understanding and controlling their thought and communication processes.

Neuro-linguistic programming (NLP), a psychological methodology, involves learning the methods used by successful people in order to achieve a specific goal. It connects concepts, terminology, and behavioural tendencies learned via experience to certain outcomes. NLP supporters think all human behaviour is positive. Therefore, it is neither good nor bad if a plan doesn't work out or if something unexpected happens; it merely adds to our knowledge about the relevant subject.

NLP (Neuro-Linguistic Programming) was first studied in the 1970s, but owing to several developers throughout the years, the area has continued to advance. The fundamental idea of this book—the NLP Communication Model—is the foundation upon which this approach to human development is built. NLP has been used by people, coaches, and mental health experts to overcome anxieties and restrictions, boost confidence, and progress toward a more successful life. It all started with the basic idea of how a person filters their views and how that influences their mind.

> *"Failure enhances your experience, success enhances your perception of yourself. Everything in life has its good aspects; you simply need to see things positively and concentrate on what you have rather than whining about what you lack."*

The originators of neuro-linguistic programming used to ponder how successful individuals are able to succeed time and time again. So they conducted studies and developed an NLP theory. They discovered that successful people began with why, what, and how, determining why they were doing something and how they would succeed at it.

All people are unique, yet you can learn a lot about someone just by looking at which of the four personality types they fall into. Once you learn to recognise them, there are widely acknowledged "categories" that a person might fit into, you can use this knowledge. By comprehending the language we use in our own thinking, neuro-linguistic programming (NLP) is a collection of approaches used to rewire our brains and behaviour.

In order to see achievement and then make it happen, a system was created in the 1970s by Americans Richard Bandler and John Grinder. Its strategy entails altering our beliefs and, subsequently, the behaviours or responses they cause. According to the NLP theory, our decisions are based on seeking pleasure and averting suffering and are tied to our evolutionary past. Our present and future are controlled by these predefined decision-making processes. Fortunately, NLP suggests that we may influence our lives by altering these ingrained tendencies. We may feel great and improve our lives. We may achieve our goals, feel good about ourselves, and enhance our interpersonal connections. In conclusion, NLP is a recipe for optimism.

> *"Thinking negatively will only result in trees that refuse to produce edible fruit. Thinking positively will always provide food for those who are willing to come to your table."*

We say, "Once a loser, always a loser." He's a mule who will not listen to reason. We gripe, "That's just the way he is. We group ourselves and other people into seemingly fixed categories and accept that we must go through life playing the hand that has been dealt to us. What if, however, this is not always the case? What if we saw ourselves and others as ships with sails raised, able to move and choose freely in the face of life's currents and winds, rather than as immovable islands in the oceans of circumstance? The truth is that learned behaviours may really be undone.

"Free yourself from false notions that were imposed on you by others to keep you imprisoned. Allow a futuristic reality to enter this area so that fresh perspectives might be gained."

The most effective technique to take control of yourself and your life before you can broaden your impact over others will then be revealed, using NLP strategies combined with those derived from the most contentious areas of brain research. You will learn how to use cutting-edge verbal and physical techniques in this outstanding book to instantly establish a strong sense of affiliation, comfort, and compatibility with almost anyone. You will have no trouble separating out the proven methods for disclosing your deepest desires from the ways to avoid piqueing their attention. How to master the art of manipulation for a successful personal life, career, and work environment. The use of NLP in your life simply means that whatever you concentrate on in your mind and the inner conversation you have in any circumstance are the outcomes of your life experiences.

- Would you like to learn how to reach your greatest potential and achieve your life goals?
- Would you like to examine the human body like a book?
- Do you aspire to manipulate people's minds as a puppeteer?
- Would you be interested in learning how certain people appear to succeed wildly in all they do?

- Do you want to discover what separates the unsuccessful from the successful?
- How might your favourite food help you accomplish your objectives?
- How your favourite superhero can lift you higher?
- How watching a specific kind of movie can set you free from phobias and pains?
- How the ideal person can mould you into the person you want to be?
- How a unique form may make you stronger and more self-assured?
- How a picture might aid in the letting go of unpleasant memories and experiences?
- How to break harmful behaviours you want to stop, along with a tonne of other information?

A Short History Of NLP

The Origins of Neuro Linguistic Programming collects the memories and ideas of some of the key figures from the very early years of NLP. Frank Pucelik and Richard Bandler attended Kresege College at the University of California, Santa Cruz, in 1971. Richard and Frank shared a strong interest in Gestalt Therapy; Richard had been working with Science and Behavior Books to transcribing and edit Fritz Perls' seminal book, The Gestalt Approach and Eyewitness to Therapy, and Frank had been working with some disaffected and drug-addicted kids as a result of his traumatic time in Vietnam. They formed a neighbourhood gestalt group and met twice a week for two to three hours, working together and experimenting with therapeutic language. Richard requested John Grinder, one of their college professors, to watch them work so that he may, perhaps, be able to dissect what they were doing that was so successful since they were beginning to produce some fantastic outcomes but were having trouble teaching their talents to others. The study they were conducting immediately intrigued John, a professor of linguistics. In due course, the three of them formalised what is now known as the Meta Model when he was able to add more structure. NLP was created. Each of the other participants, along with John and Frank, shares a unique narrative of this era of collaboration when something extraordinary was taking place in northern California. The role Gregory Bateson played is of great relevance, notably in bringing John, Richard, and Milton H. Erickson together. A fascinating and interesting read for anybody interested in NLP. A group of psychological approaches known as neurolinguistic programming has been around since the 1970s and is still well-liked by businesses and coaches.

> *"You must access the meaning of the term "comfortable" for yourself, which for you is a series of pictures, sensations, or sounds, in order to grasp what I am saying to you. The words I use are only arbitrary labels for various aspects of your own past. That is a fundamental idea of how language functions, and we refer to this activity as transderivational search. Words act as triggers, causing you to focus on some aspects of your experience while ignoring others."*

NLP offers some really sophisticated self-manipulation techniques that will enable you to master your ideas, get rid of undesirable tendencies, and eventually succeed in life. NLP relies on the idea of modelling: it's feasible to simulate the thoughts and behaviour patterns of a successful person so that others might use them as a model. You can also apply the behavioural patterns that have worked best for you to the aspects of your personality that you'd like to develop.

How does NLP work?

Using neuro-linguistic programming, you may alter someone's beliefs and actions to help them get the results you want. It may be used to treat phobias and anxiety disorders, as well as to boost productivity at work or general well-being. NLP employs perceptual, behavioural, and communicative strategies to facilitate behavioural change in individuals. NLP is dependent on language processing. However, while having the same acronym as NLP, the two are not the same. Richard Bandler and John Grinder, who thought it was feasible to recognise the thinking and behaviour patterns of successful people and impart them to others, invented NLP.

NLP is challenging to define because of the many ways it may be used. Its foundation is the assumption that humans navigate the environment using internal "maps" that they develop via sensory experiences. NLP seeks to identify and change any unintentional biases or constraints in a person's worldview. Hypnotherapy is not NLP. Instead, it works by altering someone's beliefs and behaviour via the deliberate use of words. For instance, the notion that a person is biassed toward one sensory system, known as the preferred representational system or PRS, is a key component of NLP. Language allows therapists to identify this predilection.

Key components of neurolinguistic programming are modelling, action, and successful communication. The idea is that if someone can comprehend how another person completes a task, they may copy that process and explain it to others so they, too, can complete the work. Neuro-linguistic programming proponents contend that each person has a unique map of reality. NLP practitioners examine their own and other points of view to provide a methodical picture of a situation. The NLP user learns through comprehending a variety of viewpoints. Supporters of this school of thought think that the body and mind interact and that the senses are essential for processing information. The methodology of neuro-linguistic programming is experiential. Therefore, in order to learn from an experience, one must engage in the behaviour in question in order to comprehend it.

NLP practitioners contend that learning, communication, and transformation all follow natural hierarchies. The following six logical degrees of change Involvement in something greater than oneself, such as religion, ethics, or another system, can be a sign of purpose and spirituality. This is the most significant change. Identity: Identity is the person you see yourself as, which also encompasses the duties and obligations you have in life. Beliefs and values: These are the topics that are important to you and your personal set of beliefs. Your abilities and your range of capabilities are listed below. Your unique activities are known as your behaviours. Your context or location, which includes any other individuals nearby, is known as your environment. This is the most fundamental change. Each logical level's function is to arrange and lead the information below it. Therefore, altering one level may result in altering another level. On the other hand, NLP theory states that altering a higher level will likewise affect lower ones.

Few Key Words Of NLP

PRS: A person's mental map of the world is created using information gathered from their senses. It is possible for this information to be kinesthetic, gustatory, olfactory, visual, or auditory. NLP practitioners think that each person processes events using a main representational system and that this information varies individually in terms of quality and relevance (PRS). An NLP therapist must make an effort to match a client's PRS in order to use their personal map in order to deal with them successfully. Practitioners of NLP think that signals like eye movements may be used to access representational systems. I get your reasoning. For example, it may indicate a visual "PRS". Or, saying "I hear your point" might indicate an auditory PRS. A "PRS" is identified by an NLP practitioner, who bases their therapeutic framework around it. The framework can entail developing a rapport, learning more about them, and setting goals with them.

Reframing: It's a different strategy that alters the meaning of an event by altering how you view it. Responses and actions will alter along with the meaning. You may modify the way you view the world by using words to reframe it, which alters its meaning. Jokes, myths, stories, fairy tales, and the majority of creative ways of thinking all rely on reframing. NLP's reframing strategy entails affirming the good intentions that underlie the behaviors that one wants to modify (usually an undesirable trait of behavior). Finding alternatives to meet the good intention is followed by internal discussions to resolve conflicts, examine the environment, and adopt the new behaviours. In neuro-linguistic programming, the term "reframing" is also used to indicate altering the context or depiction of an issue. In NLP, the "six-step re-frame" is one of the most efficient methods for bringing about practically any desired change. Reframing is a frequent method through which meanings are produced and lost in a variety of contexts, and it happens in life independently of NLP.

Anchoring: The concept of an "anchor" being employed in NLP jargon is noteworthy. To keep a ship or boat in one place and prevent it from drifting away, the crew members of the vessel secure the anchor to a solid object. The conclusion of this is that the signal that acts as a psychological "anchor" is more of a reference point that aids in stabilising a specific condition than it is a mechanical stimulus that "causes" a reaction. To completely apply the analogy, a ship may be thought of as our awareness's focal point on the sea of experience.

It is the process of converting sensory impressions into emotional impulses. Anchoring is a technique for actively achieving state control in which a person links a specific bodily sensation. According to NLP, we continually "anchor" (classical condition) our emotional states to what we see, hear, and feel. If a person experiences a novel stimulus (such as sight, sound, or touch) when they are experiencing an emotion, a link is created between the emotion and the novel stimulus. If the unique stimulus occurs again, the emotional state will be triggered. This kind of associative conditioning has been broadened in NLP to allow connections between experiences other than those limited to environmental cues and behavioural responses. For example, a recalled image might serve as an anchor for a certain emotional emotion. An anchor for a feeling of exhilaration or confidence might be the tone of one's voice. These connections may be created and reactivated by an individual on purpose. An anchor transforms into a tool for self-empowerment rather than being a thoughtless knee-jerk reaction. The mental processes linked to creativity, learning, focus, and other valuable resources can be established and activated with the aid of anchoring.

With the use of anchors, we may locate a specific area in this ocean of experience, retain our attention there, and prevent it from drifting. Imagine how you would feel if you could instantly transform from feeling nervous to being confident and completely capable in the middle of a nerve-wracking interview while everyone is watching you or when interacting with someone you find difficult to get along with.

Manipulation: The art of manipulation in NLP can help you become more aware of the realm of dark psychology, whatever your goal or need may be. This will provide you with an in-depth understanding of the workings of the human brain, which is a fascinating area. You'll learn how to control mind in neuro-linguistic programming, body language, and more by looking into the ideas that make up dark psychology. There may be certain instances on how to apply the techniques presented properly if you're worried about the ethical ramifications of dark psychology.

While some people think it is feasible to control one's thoughts and that it may have happened to them, others are sceptics who don't actually think it is. The fundamentals of mind control and manipulation are covered in this book. It deals with dark psychology ideas and various mind-controlling strategies, including hypnosis, persuasion, deceit, brainwashing, and manipulation. With the help of neurolinguistic programming, everything is possible! The theory behind this approach, which was created in the 1970s, is that if you can alter your language, you can change your life!

Meta Programme: Metaprogramming determines which of our senses receives our attention. Metaprogrammes are thought processes that control, drive, and regulate other thought processes. They are hence processes related to or above (meta to) the mental processes they influence. Let me use a metaphor: the programming component of NLP is what we are talking about. In essence, we model using the Meta Model and employ a variety of practical abilities to accomplish our objective. It is now possible to programme computers. Considering a computer programme and meta-programs Programs known as "meta programmes" do tasks that would typically be completed at compile time, such as writing or manipulating other programmes as data.

It is important to consider our adaptability. We are empowered to take actions that bring us closer to the very real realities of fulfilment and success as a consequence of realising the ways in which our brains and bodies either assist or impede us in a number of circumstances. If you will, picture two villages that are cut off from each other by an impassable mountain. There is no interaction or communication between them. If the brain and nervous system are represented by one town, while thinking, perception, and behaviour are represented by the other, then Meta-Programs would function as a tunnel designed to cut through the mountain, connecting the two and enabling the flow of information between them.

The salesman will always compare the car you're looking at with a less appealing car and show you the differences and how the car you're looking at is much better. He'll show you the difference in price, the mileage in the city, the safety features, etc., but always in comparison to another car, one that you didn't even consider buying. However, if you tend to find the "mismatch," or the things that are in conflict, the salesman will have to constantly compare the car you're driving currently.

Our predisposition to make decisions in a particular way is determined by the Meta-Programs. Isn't it a somewhat ambiguous statement? For instance, it will be simpler to convince you to buy a new car if the salesman demonstrates how the car's shape helps to muffle engine noise, how the automatic gear shifts smoothly with your style of driving, and how the price of the car can be divided into instalments that perfectly match your current financial capabilities.

Rapport: To strengthen communication and reaction through empathy, the practitioner tunes into the person by mimicking their bodily mannerisms. In NLP, rapport is referred to as a receptive state. Responding to you both consciously and intuitively implies that the person or individuals you are communicating with gives you the upper hand in the conversation. In NLP, mirroring is the process of adopting some physical and vocal characteristics from another person in order to establish or speed up rapport. After a time of mirroring, you shift slightly to the other person's position, who will then adopt it to maintain the symmetry that had previously existed. The other person will be less critical of your recommendations and thoughts if they are unintentionally following your example.

Swish pattern: The alteration of mental or behavioural patterns in order to achieve a desired rather than an unfavourable outcome. The swish pattern is a technique for changing a thinking pattern from one that typically results in undesirable behaviour to one that results in desired behaviour. This entails retraining the mind to "switch" to a visualisation of the desired goal, such as a healthy-looking person who is energetic and fit, and imagining a "trigger" that leads to the undesirable action, such as a smoker's hand going towards the face with a cigarette in it. In order to improve the experience, auditory effects are frequently imagined in addition to imagery.

Visual/kinesthetic dissociation (VKD): An attempt to eliminate negative memories and emotions associated with a previous experience. Visual imagery is used in VKD to examine traumatic situations from a new angle. Most of the time, events may be recreated graphically from above or from the perspective of a spectator. The rationale behind the various viewpoints is that since the person is not directly engaged, they may revisit the event in a less stressful setting. It is often referred to as the "Rewind method". Reducing traumatic memories is intended to help patients learn from their experiences and comprehend why they occurred. Major trauma or phobia sufferers like this method since the participant doesn't have to be exposed to unwanted emotions or tell the counsellor everything that happened.

Future pacing: It is the process of asking someone to imagine doing something in the future while keeping track of their responses. When someone imagines themselves in a challenging circumstance before and after an intervention, body language is often observed to determine whether the transformation process was successful. The intervention has failed if the body language remains the same. Numerous NLP strategies finish with future pacing. It is employed following a decision-destroying approach, at the conclusion of a six-step reframing, or when changing an unconscious habit. or after a shift in history. In NLP goal planning, future pacing is utilised successfully through the well-formed result process.

Approaches may be utilised for a wide range of objectives since they centre on changing behaviour. To treat depression and anxiety, mental health practitioners utilise NLP alone or in combination with other forms of treatment, such as talk therapy or psychoanalysis. It can be used to treat several forms of anxiety, including panic attacks and phobias in particular. A new map will be created by the therapist that replaces the old one with empowered routines and practical tactics. The therapist will strive to uncover the person's "map," the unproductive patterns that keep us feeling trapped.

> "*A neuro-linguistic programming (NLP) approach that involves actively attempting to manipulate someone's emotional and mental state is sometimes referred to as "state control. According to NLP, anchors may be purposefully made and activated to assist people reach "resourceful" or other goal states. An example of an anchor would be a specific identified touch connected to a memory or experience.*"

Those who are interested in personal growth—a strong human urge that may provide fulfilment to our lives—but do not have a major mental health problem may also benefit from neurolinguistic programming. Skills like public speaking, sales and negotiation, team building, and leadership may all be improved with NLP approaches. NLP and coaching work hand in hand because of its action-oriented nature and emphasis on progress. To assist their clients in rewiring their minds and achieving their goals, several coaches employ NLP approaches.

The methods of neuro-linguistic programming are the precise methods which holds that people can only perceive a small portion of the world directly using their conscious awareness and that this perception is filtered by experience, beliefs, values, assumptions, and biological sensory systems. According to NLP, people's actions and emotions are determined by how they see and feel about the world as a whole.

> *"I believe that language represents the collective knowledge of a people. From a potentially limitless range of sensory information, language selects those things that are consistent in the experience of the speakers and that they have found beneficial to pay attention to in awareness."*

According to NLP, language and behaviors—whether healthy or unhealthy—are highly organised, and this structure may be "modelled" or replicated in a way that can be repeated. The more effective aspects of one's own conduct can be "modelled" using NLP in order to be replicated in areas where one is less successful, or one can "model" another person to alter beliefs and behaviour to enhance functioning. If someone succeeds at something, it is possible to deduce exactly how they accomplish it by paying attention to some crucial behavioural cues. Hypnotic methods are one of several strategies included in NLP, according to its proponents, which may alter how individuals learn, think, and communicate.

> *"You have always been evolving, if you took the time to stop and consider your life from a little different angle."*

Life Coaches through NLP help patients comprehend their emotional condition, ambitions, and thought and behavioural patterns. The therapist can aid the patient in identifying and enhancing their greatest talents as well as in creating new techniques to replace ineffective ones by looking at the patient's mental map. Individuals in therapy may find this technique helpful in achieving their goals.

Emerging Needs Of NLP

NLP proponents assert that their methodology enhances comprehension of cognitive and behavioural patterns while delivering quick, long-lasting outcomes. In order to foster better communication between conscious and unconscious thought processes, NLP also aims to foster more creativity and problem-solving abilities in its clients. NLP has been used commercially by practitioners to achieve goals related to the workplace, such as increased productivity or career advancement. It has been used as a kind of therapy for mental illnesses such as phobias, depression, generalised anxiety disorders, and post-traumatic stress disorder. For a variety of reasons, it might be difficult to assess NLP's efficacy. NLP has not undergone the same kind of rigorous scientific testing as more well-known treatments like cognitive behavioural therapy, or CBT.

- *Why do so many sportspeople employ visualisation strategies?*
- *Why is the health and wellness movement so fond of affirmations and incantations?*
- *Why do the most prosperous businesspeople always seem to be privy to information that others are not?*

Not only their confidence, though. You might not be familiar with it, but neuro-linguistic programming techniques could be the solution. People who are successful are prepared to take risks that unsuccessful people pass up, which is what sets them apart from those who aren't. Among these is the use of NLP methods. They're an effective way to alter your outlook on life, and you can use them right away. NLP has gained a lot of popularity over time. The fact that practitioners can use it in a variety of situations and areas may have contributed to its popularity. Because NLP is based on a broad set of concepts, and because there is no institutional organisation to oversee its application, the methods and level of practise can vary greatly. In any event, convincing and unbiased proof of its efficacy is still lacking. For these reasons, it's probable that effective marketing has also aided in NLP's widespread acceptance, particularly in the business world.

> *"The field of neuro-linguistic programming investigates how our ideas influence our actions. It examines how our brains perceive messages and how these interpretations influence our actions."*

The linguistic component of neuro-linguistic programming approaches is how it does this. NLP approaches assist us in viewing our thoughts, feelings, and emotions as things we can influence rather than as things that passively happen to us by looking at how our brains process information. Due to the absence of formal regulation and its financial value, claims of NLP's efficacy might be based on anecdotal evidence or information provided by an NLP provider. The success of NLP will be in the financial interests of NLP suppliers, making it challenging to trust their data. Furthermore, there have been conflicting findings from scientific studies on NLP.

We may better understand and appreciate the diversity in how people interact with and react to their environment by being aware of the Meta-Programs. Understanding Meta-Programs enables us to modify our own behaviours and responses in ways that match and complement their own, rather than viewing these differences as impediments or irritants. Therefore, meta-programs are helpful in bridging gaps in knowledge and in fostering cooperation and synergy. Meta-Programs might help teachers engage their pupils more successfully. They might help police officers diffuse tense situations more effectively. Parents who need to reprimand their children and want to encourage desired conduct would benefit from using meta-programs.

It's also important to note that the majority of research on NLP's usefulness in business settings has been done in therapeutic contexts. Certain research has linked NLP advantages to certain For instance, compared to a control group, psychotherapy patients had improved psychiatric symptoms and life quality after receiving NLP, according to a study published in the journal Counselling and Psychotherapy Research.

"While having existed for more than 40 years, neither the efficacy of NLP nor the truthfulness of the ideas have been amply supported by credible research. Additionally, there are a number of practical difficulties in studying how effectively NLP functions, which adds to the haziness around the topic. Given the variety of diverse approaches, procedures, and results, it is challenging, for instance, to compare research side by side."- Dr. Amit Das

Build Self-Confidence And Boost Your Performance

"Remember, it's your own body, your own brain. You're not a victim of the universe, you are the universe."— Richard Bandler

How to build self-confidence, live a purposeful life, and outperform?

We frequently hear that practise makes perfect, but a new study of more than 11,000 people discovered that this is not the case. Deliberate practise only accounted for roughly 1% of your performance. For instance, improving as a programmer does not merely come from using a language over and over again. The problem is that while the majority of successful people would claim that they achieved their objectives via consistent practice, people who have tried repeatedly yet failed to achieve anything are never mentioned. Your brain has to be active and well rested for purposeful practise to be effective. How, therefore, may intentional practise be optimised? You must first care about what you are doing.

What could you do to increase your interest in any activity?

Your brain's motivational areas will naturally activate as a result. Additionally, take a breather after each mistake you make to avoid repeating them. As you can see, perseverance and careful practise do not ensure success in the workplace. Your brain will become less of an automaton and you will have a better chance of overcoming challenging tasks at work if you have faith in your task, consider if change is required, care about what you are doing, and take care not to repeat mistakes. When your confidence is damaged, you might assume that you'll just have to wait to feel better. However, there are techniques you can do to quickly boost your confidence by focusing on your brain.

Let's go through three strategies to rewire your brain to feel more in control at work when you lack confidence. The first method is based on a notion put forth by Daniel Wegner, a Harvard psychologist. He discovered that urging yourself not to do something while you're under stress causes your brain to operate in the exact opposite way. For instance, if you tell yourself, "I will not munch on the workplace chocolates," you will really do just that. That's because your brain doesn't have the capacity to control your tension, advance you, and stop you from acting all at once.

It seems as though it is deaf to the word not. Therefore, you must define your objective without using the verb "do not." Another way of framing it favourably Say, "I will consume nutritious snacks," as opposed to, "I will not munch on the sweets." Varun was a coaching client of mine once. One or two people on Varun's team truly irritated him when he served as Team Lead for an advertising firm. He would frequently remind himself, "Don't lose your anger," before team meetings, but when he was there, he would lose his cool. I thus informed Varun about the brain's insensitivity to the word "not". Instead, I advised him to convince himself to "be calm." He changed this, and it worked.

The second approach is referred to as "Affect labelling". Affect refers to feelings. When you label an emotion, you describe it. Simply said, it implies that you can name every emotion as it arises. Saying "I'm anxious" will help your brain relax if, for instance, worry is destroying your confidence. Leaving your emotions unnamed and unchecked just makes you feel more nervous.

The third technique involves talking to yourself in a way that makes you feel energised. For instance, Varun used to remark, "I'm going to crush this," before team meetings, but studies have discovered that Varun should add, "Varun, you're going to crush this." You see, calling oneself by name and speaking to yourself in the second or third person helps you feel less scared and has a positive impact on your ability to manage your emotions.

> "*In fact, your brain reacts by helping you better manage your emotions even when you're not trying. So refrain from using the word not to aid your brain in boosting your confidence. Start by recognising the sensation you are experiencing right now, then give yourself a boost in the manner I've just explained, and try it out at your next team meeting.*"

Creating a sense of purpose in your life can help your brain become more motivated. Your brain has a limited amount of motivational strength, and as you age, some of this ability may wane. But did you know that having a feeling of purpose in life can have positive effects on your brain that can speed up the process of achieving your goals?

Do you have a specific purpose in your life?

Let's examine what it means to have a feeling of purpose and how your brain is impacted by it. I'll then examine how these brain modifications might enhance your productivity at work. People sometimes confuse feeling a sense of purpose with working for a cause or a group of people, but that is not what it entails. Aristotle, a philosopher, said that having a sense of purpose simply implies that you are motivated by the nature of your activity. As a result, you don't need to exert extra effort to achieve your goals. For instance, one of your responsibilities could be to assist the company's CEO. This goes beyond a sense of direction. Instead, you could get a rush from the arranging you do for me. You carry out the task only to fulfil that sense of purpose.

> *"In reality, having a sense of purpose is more about how you feel than what you desire. Setting aside time to think critically about this is what it is. Asking yourself who or what you want to serve is counterproductive. Instead, consider what you actually like, what comes naturally and effortlessly, and what you will continue to enjoy no matter what."*

The brain is impacted by purpose in many different ways. First, it triggers the brain's reward region, much like your favourite song or dish does. The default mode network is then activated in the brain. You feel more creative and self-connected thanks to this network. This goes beyond a feeling of direction. Instead, you could get a rush from the arranging you do for me. You carry out the task only to fulfil that sense of purpose. The brain is impacted by purpose in many different ways. First, it triggers the brain's reward region, much like your favourite song or dish does. The default mode network is then activated in the brain. You feel more creative and self-connected thanks to this network. Finally, having a feeling of purpose shields your brain from stressful situations and speeds up recovery. This makes me think of a customer I once had by the name of Zumbaa, whose fitness company failed. Her life was in constant chaos, and at first she had no clue how she was going to get well. But Zumbaa was able to quickly recover, nevertheless, because of her sense of purpose.

I asked her questions based on her brain to reawaken her feeling of purpose. To activate her reward centre, I asked her what she truly enjoyed doing rather than who or what she wanted to serve. Then, in order to open up her brain's creative circuit, I asked her what made her feel the most like herself. I finally questioned her about the easiest and most natural way to focus on the good. Zumbaa returned to business within a month, as opposed to other clients who took more than a year to do so. Although her fitness firm may have failed, she felt a renewed sense of purpose. Keep a diary for this purpose and record your responses. Check back on it every month or every three months to see whether your responses have changed or stayed the same. Your sense of purpose will remain alive thanks to this activity.

What can professionals do to begin using brain-based concepts at work, and how might brain-based principles affect how they think about their practises?

There are four crucial ways that neuroscience might be beneficial. It can enhance the way learning professionals create their training materials, deepen their understanding of why soft skills are important, disprove their outdated coaching techniques that may seem logical at first, but do not follow biological logic, and add subtleties that have a significant impact on learning and leadership outcomes. When learning professionals ask what significant improvement I would make to their learning curriculam, I suggest including more learning that has an influence on the unconscious brain. You see, more than 90% of everything your brain does takes place unconsciously. So why devote all of your learning budget to conscious tools and strategies? After all, that would only improve 10% of your brain's functionality.

> *"According to Gartner, a renowned provider of business research, by 2021, 25% of businesses will use neuroscience to improve individual development. And the addition of neuroscience to the minds of those who are committed to learning and leadership development may greatly improve their work-based practises."*

For instance, there are significant unconscious components in decision-making, intuition, and creativity. Doodling is a straightforward exercise that can increase memory by 29% and have an effect on the unconscious mind. It's possible that practising this form of decision-making is even more crucial than learning how to be more intuitive or creative.

Brain research significantly contributes to comprehending at a deeper level.

A management team of engineers and I previously collaborated. They struggled to comprehend the necessity for greater empathy in order to connect with their staff. But when scientists discovered that empathy, a soft talent, could alter both their own and other people's brains, they concluded that soft skills might also have real-world repercussions. Numerous outdated procedures still exist and are occasionally incorrect. Brain research can assist in dispelling misconceptions. For instance, some managers who also coach teams think it's important to constantly monitor performance in relation to objectives.

> *"According to a current study, the brain releases too much adrenaline when objectives are continually being tracked. People who take too much adrenaline experience extreme anxiety or even paralysis. They move more slowly as a result."*

Finally, there are several outdated techniques that fail to take into account the subtleties of how the brain works. Nowadays, it's a popular notion that feedback is ineffective since it increases resistance and anxiety in individuals. In other workplaces, 360-degree feedback systems have even been totally eliminated. While there is some benefit in this, a new study demonstrates that, depending on how it is given and understood, even negative feedback may be beneficial. On the one hand, when providing feedback, you don't want to shock or demotivate the brain. But the brain might also pick up new information when someone else points out a mistake.

If you work in learning and leadership development, neuroscience may be a great asset since it can explain unconscious learning, support soft skill training with biological justifications, and reexamine time-honored conventions. The study of the brain can help you improve your existing strategy. Many people believe that tenacity and purposeful practise are the cornerstones of effort and excellence, but a new study raises the possibility that this may not be the case at all.

Let's talk about why grit and purposeful practise aren't as effective as we would think they are at improving work performance, how the brain plays a role, and how to best utilise both. Grit is a term that describes two characteristics: persistence and consistency, or how persistently and consistently someone works on a subject. For instance, having grit indicates that you won't give up and will keep doing the same thing if your sales statistics fall short of your objective. Even while persistence and consistency seem like positive traits, they will barely have any effect on your sales figures.

A hint as to why this is the case comes from brain research. People with grit have brains that are wired for persistence and consistency, but having a growth mindset is also necessary for the perseverance and consistency switches in the brain to be activated. In other words, people have to think they can improve. This notion is essential. The grit will be useless without this conviction. Additionally, it's foolish to wage a futile struggle. If all you have to succeed is grit, you'll be squandering your time if you have a narrow focus. Periodically, you must confirm that you are moving in the proper direction.

Many individuals choose to persist when it would be better to change their direction. Consequently, if you're holed up at your desk working, do the following: First, be certain that you think you can achieve your goal. If not, your perseverance won't amount to anything. Then, pause sometimes to decide if you should continue on your current path or choose a different one. Put a strategy on hold for a week or do this over the course of a day. When you do, you'll enable your brain's "grit circuits" to support improved performance at work.

How to rewire your brain for better work focus?

When you're not paying attention, you could assume that staying there and pushing through is enough, but this is frequently not the case. What causes our minds to wander, and what can we do to prevent this? Let's look at this now. Your brain might become less concentrated due to a variety of factors. These include emotional exhaustion, information overload, and information that is too ambiguous. You lose attention when you're emotionally drained by dread or even excessive enthusiasm. This is so because your brain's concentrated regions and emotional processing areas are connected. Therefore, while your brain's emotional alarms are sounding, it also impairs your ability to concentrate. When you have trouble concentrating, consider whether an emotion could be interfering with your ability to pay attention.

Are you concerned or enraged?

Make every effort to address it after you've identified what it is. The brain confusion created by unpleasant emotions can be reduced and concentration can be improved by simply labelling the feelings, such as anger or sadness. You have reached your brain's limit if there is too much information distracting you. More information, particularly material that might distract you, cannot be stored. Imagine that you are at work. You receive many distressing texts from pals during the course of the day, in addition to an email from your employer and a warning from your bank that your finances are low. You seem to have more and more on your plate as each hour goes by. Your brain will then store this knowledge, but it will appear that everything has to be done at once. Your brain becomes overloaded with information as a result, making it difficult to concentrate on anything at all. Put each activity on your calendar and prioritise it to help you focus more.

When will you get back to your boss?

You don't have to respond to all of these requests for contact just because they come in at the same time. It will make you feel less overwhelmed with knowledge if you allot a specific amount of time for each activity. Last but not least, hazy information might be annoying. Uncertainty causes our minds to become uneasy. You must thus define things more precisely. Imagine you have a group of individuals anticipating a new merger. Tell them exactly what to anticipate and when to expect it, or mention that you have a team of individuals that have fallen short of the quarterly targets. Tell them both the best and worst case possibilities in this situation.

You shouldn't just leave folks hanging in any scenario. Give them as much information as you can so they won't be preoccupied with anxiety. So, as you can see, your brain can be disturbed by emotions, an abundance of information, and ambiguous information, but if you take measures to stop these disturbances, your brain will be better able to focus. You shouldn't just leave folks hanging in any scenario. Give them as much information as you can so they won't be preoccupied with anxiety. So, as you can see, your brain can be disturbed by emotions, an abundance of information, and ambiguous information, but if you take measures to stop these disturbances, your brain will be better able to focus.

> *"There is a lot of ambiguity at work. You can be confused by a new position, a new digital platform, or new leadership. Although it can seem as though you must deal with this uncertainty, you need not. Your brain can be altered to handle this."*

Let's talk about the effects of uncertainty on your psychology and brain, as well as what you can do to alter your brain to better manage ambiguity. I once collaborated with a food and beverage company's executive team. Recently, one of their rivals took some of their market share, and as a result, their earnings fell. They were upset by this and requested my assistance in developing a mindset plan to help them get back on track and reclaim their market share. And because I could tell they were unsure, I told them we needed to deal with this right away. You see, your brain warps how you perceive things when you're uncertain. You're unable to think clearly as a result of that.

According to a specific study, 75% of individuals think something horrible is about to happen, even when it isn't. It's known as "negative bias". When someone is typically worried, their tendency toward negativity might be considerably stronger. Almost always in life, you prepare for the worst. This unwarranted sense of fear that arises with uncertainty is the result of several brain processes happening simultaneously. Your brain's processing of conflict and anxiety overreacts, which causes you to feel sick to your stomach because your brain's area that records gut emotions is also overactive. You lose the capacity to appropriately see reality because your emotional brain is working overtime.

> *"It seems as though you are viewing everything in reality through a dark lens. Therefore, your strategies might not be successful. You have two options for controlling the distortion that uncertainty produces. Start by telling yourself aloud or silently in your thoughts."*

Uncertainty causes my brain to overreact. It is quite gloomy. Then you can respond, "Knowing what's coming doesn't always imply anything bad will happen; it just implies I don't know," or anything along those lines. By doing this, you will reset your brain from negative to neutral. Include tasks that you have control over on your to-do list, if you have one. Consider finishing the report if you can or taking periodic breaks. If you inject a little certainty into your days, they'll feel safer. Uncertainty might confuse your brain, but you can calm it down by using self-talk and taking charge of the things you can control.

For example, brain-based activities can help you improve your decision-making, resilience, agility, and soft skills. Additionally, it may be used to boost confidence, develop a team, and quicken strategy. Keep a notebook nearby and jot down any important information as you watch each video to make it easier to remember and put the advice into practise. You will have a completely new toolset to handle difficulties at work once you discover how to modify your brain. When you do, you may also make these tools available to others or share them with your team members.

When things aren't going well at work, we all experience stress, uncertainty, disagreements, and a loss of confidence. Normally, we try to solve these problems without thinking about the brain, but what if you could change your brain so that, no matter what the problem, you could feel better and perform better at work? I'll draw on my experience as a certified psychologist, educator, counsellor, and executive coach in this book to show you how to rewire your brain so that you feel better and perform at your best. Peak performance in the workplace refers to your mental and physical condition when you are performing at your highest level. According to what I know about the human brain, there are three questions that workers should ask themselves to help them feel motivated and in sync.

- *How much value do you place on the work that you do?*
- *Does the job fit with who you are?*
- *And do you feel like you have enough control?*

For instance, I've previously collaborated with a leadership group at a non profit organisation. For the purpose of boosting the team's motivation, the leader recruited me. I probed the team as to why they value their job rather than only motivating them in the near term. And if they thought their positions were a good fit for them. They began to become more motivated as they gave it more thought. After that, we created software to give them a sense of control. This featured musings, communication strategies, and discoveries based on the brain. As an executive coach, I frequently assist clients who are facing challenging situations at work. They can change how their brains process the difficulty, but they can't change their work environments. Let's examine how I know that you can alter your brain and how we know that brain transformation is feasible. I'll also look at how you might use brain indicators for both personal and social benefit.

A leadership team in human resources that I formerly worked with was extremely overworked, and there were no indicators that the task was becoming any lighter. They asked me for assistance. I mentioned that although there wasn't much they could do about the burden, they could alter their brains to handle it better. There is evidence for this from extensive studies. Your brain, for instance, has the capacity to create new neuronal connections as well as new neuronal cells. Your new brain may be able to manage obstacles more skillfully because of both of these modifications.

You can alter your brain, which is incredible. Brain scans allow us to compare the state of your brain before and after you make a behavioural or mental shift. Thanks to the scans, you will be able to see in detail how the brain has altered after the behaviour or mindset adjustment takes effect. For instance, a brain scan may reveal that a particular brain area has grown or shrunk. Additionally, it can demonstrate how regional and interregional variations in brain blood flow occur. Increased or decreased cerebral blood flow often indicates that a particular area of the brain is being used more or less and that the brain tissue in that area is also changing how it operates.

For instance, when you're exhausted, doing straightforward things like getting more rest, listening to music, reducing your stress, improving your diet, or altering your thinking in particular ways can all have a great impact on your brain. And when it occurs, you can also perform better at work. Do not misunderstand; you do not need to have brain scans each time you encounter a professional obstacle.

Do you know that employee engagement may also be improved via brain science?

By assisting individuals in understanding what the brain is preventing them from doing when they want to do something but are unable to. For instance, there are two different types of intent. Intentions for achieving goals and carrying them out Intentions for goals are more broad. I aim to complete the last of my tasks on time, for instance. Implementation intentions entail identifying the project you want to complete as well as the precise time, day, and date you intend to do so. Brain research can aid in optimum performance by establishing a link between human behaviour and brain function. They engage in brain-based activities to accomplish their objectives after they learn how to alter their brains in order to alter their behaviour. Additionally, brain-based coaching tools may teach you how to optimise your brain for this.

How could coaching tools based on the brain provide special benefits for businesses?

Utilising brain-based technologies in your company can help you gain a better understanding of why certain operations are successful or unsuccessful. Align the actions of the workforce with the company's strategy. and raises both consumer and staff engagement. For instance, one realisation is the fact that mental calmness can result from distraction. Instead of waiting with baited breath outside your team leader's office for criticism, you can browse your Instagram account to pass the time. Similar to this, when employees aren't on board with the company's plan, we could investigate the reasons for their declining motivation.

People with prejudice also have particularly conflict-sensitive brains, and they find differences repugnant. Therefore, the conflict and disgust brain areas will engage if someone feels torn about incorporating a new team member or is otherwise repulsed by their manner, possibly because they are too effeminate. According to researchers, we frequently dread others who are unlike us. And whenever we do, we leave them out. It is possible that you will be unaware of this when it occurs, but this fear may cause you to exclude qualified individuals due to your biases. You are biassed for more reasons besides just fear. Additionally, they'll harbour prejudices towards that individual. Prejudice also damages our own minds and lives.

How do you then manage your prejudices?

Start by challenging any strong feelings you may have for someone. Prejudices are exactly what gut responses are. Then keep in mind that you're more likely to be prejudiced if you just get through your day without stopping. It helps to have sufficient cognitive power to regulate your thoughts in order to lessen bias. You should schedule breaks throughout your day because of this. You can get one to three hours of clarity from five to fifteen minutes of napping. And taking regular naps will continually reenergise your brain.

Finally, being conscious of your worries might be beneficial. Talk to your team if you have any fears about particular racial groups, genders, personality types, or age groups. In order for team members to feel comfortable discussing their concerns and biases in team meetings, leaders should work to provide an environment that is safe and open for expression. After all, bias exists in all of us, sometimes unknowingly. People will be able to modify their prejudices and not hide them if they are aware of this. Recognise that your brain could overreact to someone's distaste when they accuse you of bias. Instead of thinking about how to react to them, ask yourself, "How can I see the world through their eyes?" As you can see, prejudice may stand in the way of diversity, but you can work to reduce your prejudice, choose diverse team members, and take care of your own brain by ensuring that it has enough energy and overcoming your concerns.

Did you know that bias against people based on their age, gender, skin color, ethnicity, or personality traits begins in their brains, even if they are unaware of it? It is therefore beneficial to comprehend what goes on in the unconscious mind covertly. By doing so, you may broaden the scope of your decisions and enhance team performance.

Let's examine how prejudice affects the brain and how you might lessen your prejudice to make judgments at work that are more objective. In this way, you might benefit from many viewpoints, styles, and ideas. The amygdala, a part of the brain responsible for processing fear and other emotions, becomes overactive when you have prejudices. We must constantly assess potential biases since they might be accidental or automated. I once collaborated with a group of male executives who made it very apparent that they valued women. However, they exchanged a few puzzled looks with one another when I asked them why there were no women on the squad. While they all insisted that it wasn't an intentional choice, our subsequent investigation revealed various probable biases.

We shouldn't make rash judgments based on emotions, several males stated. Others commented on how effectively they functioned as a team, so if it isn't broken, don't repair it. When I dug further, they discovered they'd made certain assumptions that weren't accurate; that there were probably many women who wouldn't be too emotional for the team; and that they were keeping things the way they were only because they were frightened of change. They made a conscious decision to include qualified women on the senior leadership team after realising this.

When your brain is constantly changing, it seems like you're in a whirlwind. If it's not the newest social media platform, a revised work procedure, or a shift in the company's strategy, There is always something to get used to. Let's look at how you can alter your brain to manage change effectively. It's crucial to understand what occurs in your brain when you cope with change. I recently collaborated with a pharmaceutical company's executive team. They were in charge of a digital transformation programme and discovered that the workforce was particularly resistant to change. The business was managing workflow and fostering cooperation with the help of a new team management software. Instead, individuals dug in their heels and resisted any more changes. Leadership was interested in learning how to motivate teams to use the new platform.

Each person's lack of confidence takes many forms. In a spiderman-like manner, we frequently tell ourselves, "I can't do it." Or we envision how miserably we will fail. Maybe we may go back to a period when we were simply informed that we weren't good enough or that we were being tormented at school. Whatever our method, the end consequence is always an emotion: a sensation of unease, trepidation, and sometimes even worry. As each concept is thought, so are the feelings. As we say in NLP, the trick is having the ability to instantly enter another emotional state. If I couldn't significantly alter my emotional state as an NLP trainer, I wouldn't be as successful or efficient.

The brain is unable to distinguish between what is real and what is imagined. Have you ever paced the room at night, fuming at someone because you imagined a fight that "maybe" might happen the next day? If the brain is capable of that, you might want to put it to use for something more constructive. How about visualising a fantastic result that makes you feel good? That is the primary use of NLP. So picture yourself travelling into the future, when the activity you don't feel quite comfortable with has ended and you've benefited much from it. See, hear, and experience everything as though it were right now. As though you are observing yourself. Have you ever noticed how quickly your emotions can change? That is correct!

Another advantage of using this strategy is that it prepares your mind for a well-formed result. What you think about becomes you! As a Life Coach, I frequently witness my clients doing this. We frequently see events as though they are happening to us right now while we are feeling an emotion over something that hasn't even occurred yet. In every way, we experience the scenario just as we would in real life. I would advise picturing the following: Your emotions are within that individual, as you may truly see yourself by floating your consciousness outside of your body. There is no feeling, as seen from this vantage point, while you observe yourself over there. You've been detached. Imagine a plexiglass wall separating you from the circumstances to increase the force of the detachment. You may even use a teflon shield to guard yourself. Thus, NLP offers a wide range of additional approaches for overcoming difficulties with self-doubt and confidence.

I urged them to inform their teams that any new adjustments would likely seem uncomfortable, even if they weren't. This is due to cognitive dissonance, a state of mental confusion brought on by change. It appears as though the brain has an alarm that won't go off when brain turmoil stimulates the conflict detector in the brain. There are a few stages to talk through in order to control this mental turbulence. First, identify the emotional cost of change that you must bear. This is the changeover cost. Instead, individuals dug in their heels and resisted any more changes. Leadership was interested in learning how to motivate teams to use the new platform. I urged them to inform their teams that any new adjustments would likely seem uncomfortable, even if they weren't. This is due to cognitive dissonance, a state of mental confusion brought on by change. It appears as though the brain has an alarm that won't go off when brain turmoil stimulates the conflict detector in the brain.

"You pay the price in the form of doubt, anxiety, and unfamiliarity. Your brain will understand that these are important even if unpleasant feelings when you convince yourself that you are willing to pay this emotional cost. Use the spreading of alternatives strategy next. It seems difficult, but it's really fairly straightforward."- Dr. Amit Das

CHAPTER THREE

Facilitating Learning Intelligence Through NLP

"The brain can be developed just the same as the muscles can be developed, if on will only take the pains to train the mind to think." -Thomas A. Edison

Utilising NLP techniques as tools for facilitating learning

Making learning memorable how much of what you learnt the day before do you still recall when you get up? Take a guess since it has been discovered that guessing, even if you guess incorrectly, improves memory for the answer. If people don't make an attempt to remember, they will forget 80% of what they learned the next day. Fortunately, there are several things you can do to increase the effectiveness of your training. With a guessing game, I'll investigate what makes objects sticky. You'll see several illustrations of the components of sticky learning, and you'll have to infer what they signify. These universal problems—bored learners, an overload of knowledge, or a particularly dull subject that you yourself find uninteresting—are something we all face.

Knowledge and learning capacities enable businesses to detect and assimilate new knowledge, apply it toward new goals, and continuously create and recreate gestalts and logical structures in organisational memory. Because they can build on and produce new knowledge, which is essential for strategy renewal, businesses with strong knowledge and learning capacities may be more inventive and adaptable. If organisations want to develop and remain competitive, managing knowledge and learning capacities becomes essential. Neuro-linguistic programming is one technique for enhancing knowledge and learning capacities (NLP).

Do you want personal growth hard enough to make an investment in yourself? One thing is certain: if you don't take action to further your personal growth, neither you nor your life will change much. The decision is yours. Do you love personal growth and striving to be your best self? Want to develop, learn, grow, and accomplish your goals? Are you looking for techniques to alter your perspective in order to get better results? What can you do to obtain clarity, let go of what's getting in your way, and silence your inner critic? Tired of merely existing and "dealing" with events as they occur? NLP is for you if you answered "Yes" to any of the following questions and are prepared to act and make a change.

Personal development is all about becoming the best version of yourself so that you can live a happy life and achieve your goals! Over the years, NLP has assisted countless numbers of devotees of personal development in their advancement. We develop a complicated web of ideas, presumptions, and attitudes about ourselves starting in childhood that govern and influence our daily lives. Numerous of them are so engrained that we spend the most of our waking hours fully oblivious of them. Some of these ideas come from the culture in which we were raised, while others are the result of our own peculiar invention.

Most of the time, we are ignorant of some of these fundamental beliefs until they are questioned, at which point we frequently erupt into an otherwise incomprehensible protective anger. When combined, a person's beliefs make up their own worldview, a web of presumptions through which we understand and filter the world around us. Every idea restricts our behaviour in some manner, and many of them are beneficial. However, certain ideas encourage harmful behaviours that have a detrimental impact on how we think and relate to others.To reprogram your belief system and alter your worldview in order to behave more positively within it, NLP provides an effective toolkit.

If the first stage of any personal development is determining where you want to go and developing your own distinct vision, the next step is to recognise where you are right now. From here, you may determine which areas of your talents and abilities can probably benefit from some improvement. You may start to address your shortcomings by taking action once you are aware of them. NLP is a dynamic, generative learning process that offers countless opportunities for improvement and development. It is a talent that never goes out of style and will develop as you do, enabling you to design experiences that fit your screenplay. A formal education that will alter both your life and the lives of people you know. Every person who practises and teaches NLP develops a special personal instrument out of this universal talent. I have a solid, realistic, and dynamic strategy for living a very successful life.

What personal development will take place when you learn NLP?

- It will help you master your emotions, think clearly and forcefully, and acquire practical skills and practises that will keep you going ahead.
- It will show you many methods for coming up with original answers to difficult problems.
- It helps you think of out-of-the-box solutions.
- You will gain a deeper grasp of your special talents and skills, as well as practical applications for them.
- It will strengthen your professional and personal connections as well as your communication skills.
- It will also open up countless options for you to find your purpose and live a meaningful life.
- It will help you gain a great deal of confidence in your capacity to make decisions, hold firm to your convictions, and adjust to your ever-changing surroundings.
- NLP provides highly powerful and effective tools to help decide what is "useful" and "not" in your life.
- NLP provides highly powerful and effective tools.
- NLP fosters a deep awareness of the verbal and nonverbal cues we all use to communicate. And trust me when I say that it will give you a good outlook on life and success in any area of emphasis. To "unstick" oneself and others and keep life going in constructive and beneficial ways, NLP includes tools and approaches that have been proved effective.

- Through NLP, liberation from the snares of conditioned reactions and outdated ideas is provided through NLP.

You'll observe that there are several options and possibilities. There are several straightforward exercises that coaches have created to help people overcome anxiety and stop self-defeating behaviour. In essence, you will graduate from training with a personal commitment to leading a "quality" life as well as the knowledge and abilities necessary to find success wherever you go for it.

What difficulties do you now have in developing and delivering your training?

I'll give you a moment to come up with some ideas on your own. Make a note of all the aspects of training that keep you up at night, or even create a mental map. Here's an illustration of how your learner's brain could function to produce some of those difficulties: Understanding a mechanism frequently aids in problem solving. First, the response of your brainstem to the circumstances. What serves your brainstem, if anything? It keeps you alive, controls sleep, and keeps an eye on your breathing, heart rate, thirst, and hunger. It is simple and adverbial. It states that I'm very hungry. What about your limbic system, which is located in the centre of your brain and is where your hippocampus processes memories subconsciously? It recalls the previous training session where there was chocolate. But your amygdala, which is a component of your limbic system and is responsible for processing a substantial portion of your emotions, links memories and emotions and is quite impulsive. It's experiencing joy.

But what about your cortex, the part of your brain responsible for conscious thought? You're aware that it is divided into two hemispheres. The left hemisphere is said to function well with my intricate descriptions and analyses of neuroscience since it handles details. Yes, neuroscience makes a lot of sense. Your right hemisphere, which prefers the grand picture and the essence of a concept, is having difficulty absorbing all of this information. It may be creative as well as a little gloomy, building enormous concepts out of small pieces of knowledge. It speaks after hearing the information coming from the rest of the brain.

Links encourage learning since that is how the human brain functions. Your brain's 86 billion neurons work together to guarantee that you can tie your shoes, compute your taxes, and converse effectively—possibly all at once. Whether you acquire a new behaviour, skill, piece of information, or habit, you are building connections between various brain regions. Totally new paths require a lot of energy to create. Your brain consumes 20% of your body's energy, so it will be a lot simpler if you can take shortcuts and rely on certain pre-existing networks. Let's examine the networks in your brain right now.

How much of your brain is currently focused on me?

You're right; very little of it since each component is oblivious to what matters to it and is instead preoccupied. Your left and right brain are linked and constantly interact with one another by a large bundle of nerves called the corpus callosum, so things just got more difficult. The majority of the chatter in your brain right now is all about chocolate since your left and right hemispheres both understand what is going on on the other side. This message is heard by the left side, which is also aware of a fun fact regarding chocolate. - Serotonin, which is found in chocolate, aids with persistence. Let's find out how much of your brain is now devoted to neuroscience.

You can persevere a lot better thanks to serotonin. I enjoy chocolate. Almost everyone is more interested in chocolate than in my amazing discussion about neuroplasticity. What does this indicate about L&D and you? Consider the difficulties you identified at the start of this video. How many could be brought on by someone's entire brain not contributing positively to the process? They could be distracted by their surroundings, either literally or psychologically. They might not be emotionally invested. They are bored, but their emotions are pulling them in another direction. It may be difficult for them to make connections between what they already know and what they are learning. Or sometimes there is too much information and not enough context, overall view, or directional cues. It is your responsibility to create learning that complements rather than competes with the way our minds are built for learning. And never forget to appreciate your brain's effort.

Is busting learning misconceptions a challenge?

Like everyone else, L&D professionals need to be at the top of our game by utilising the most recent research information and experimenting with what works and what doesn't. While neuroscience and psychology provide insightful information, they may also be difficult to understand, and scientific articles are infamous for their poor writing. The lack of scientific training and our reliance on condensed secondary sources in L&D can lead to misconceptions, subpar behaviour, and occasionally even cynicism toward effective evidence-based practise. Take this quiz to discover how many misconceptions you can dispel. I welcome you to participate. Before you begin, there is something crucial you should be aware of.

A hard arithmetic issue, for instance, could seem logical and left-brained to you, but it turns out that your brain processes little numbers on the right side and huge numbers on the left. Additionally, both the left and right sides of your mouth must talk if you need to convey information to another person. The left/right brain myth developed in large part from misconceptions regarding several antiquated theories of language processing.

I'm going to discuss five typical misconceptions regarding your learning, and your other students will guess the correct response and mark it with a red or green card depending on whether they believe it to be true or false. Please join in with their game; by guessing, you will get knowledge. First place People who are creative use their right brains, whereas logical people use their left brains. Myth or true? Congrats on your guess. You require both hemispheres of your brain, which constantly collaborate and are connected by a communication superhighway known as the corpus callosum, for everything you accomplish in the present world.

> *"Creative people utilise their right brains, whereas logical people use their left. This is untrue. Both hemispheres of your brain, which constantly collaborate and are linked by a "communication superhighway" known as the corpus callosum, are required for everything you perform in the real world."*

According to research, you are more likely to remember an answer if you guess it than if you are just told, even if you are incorrect. There is no right or incorrect answer on this quiz; the goal is to help your knowledge stick. I'm going to discuss five typical misconceptions regarding your learning, and your other students will guess the correct response and mark it with a red or green card depending on whether they believe it to be true or false.

Only about 10% of your brain is used. How do you feel if I delete the unnecessary 90% if it's true that you only utilise 10%? It's untrue. Because your brain is too energy-hungry to squander resources on inactive portions, you must employ all of them. If any part of it were not being used, it would have withered away and vanished. This myth most likely developed because there is a certain amount of brain growth that can be accomplished. Although you still use all of your brain, if one area is developed more, it may come at the expense of another.

Reading and underlining important information will help you learn and review. It is, sadly, a myth. To get your brain's neural networks to fire and connect, you need to repeatedly recollect the material you're attempting to learn. Reading fosters recognition and familiarity, which are misleading learning allies. You're better off taking your own notes or utilising mind maps to graphically represent important concepts.

When you're an adult, exercise helps you create new brain cells. This is true. Once you reach maturity, scientists used to think you couldn't generate new brain cells, but current study demonstrates a variety of brain regions, including The hippocampus, your memory centre, is one brain location that consistently produces new brain cells, contrary to what scientists formerly thought. This goes against the conventional wisdom that once you reach maturity, you can no longer generate new brain cells. And one of the most effective ways to produce BDNF(Brain Derived Neurotrophic Factor), which acts as fertiliser for your brain cells, is through exercise.

The idea that attending lectures is an effective method of learning is also untrue. There are a lot more effective methods to learn than just listening to someone go through a bunch of slides, even if many individuals can and finally do learn through the medium of lectures. As a result of your experiences with lectures and presentations, as well as the differences between lectures and active, interactive learning in which you participate, you already know this. There are far more effective ways to learn than simply listening to someone go through a bunch of slides, even if many individuals can and do learn through the medium of lectures. As a result of your experiences with lectures and presentations, as well as the differences between lectures and the active, interactive learning in which you participate, you already know this.

For instance, you could be educating someone who claims to have weak presentation abilities. They hunch their shoulders, as you can see. Encourage them to deliberately practise standing up straight and vocal exercises to improve their voice. They merely need to stand tall the next time to immediately have a louder voice. All canines can learn new skills because of the neuroplasticity of their brains, but it does take practise. Because you instinctively associate the physical and emotional surroundings with the learning while working, learning on the job is a potent linking strategy. If you can't educate someone while they're working, encourage ties back to the workplace through realistic posters, films, situations, or by having them picture themselves performing the new skills while they're working. Contextual learning is strengthened through modelling, role playing, actors, comparable noises, and emotional content. Oh sure, that's wise advice. Since smell is a powerful memory aid, link a specific fragrance to a certain topic. For instance, people can use scented tissues to acquire new information and then bring the tissue with them to an exam to help them recall it more quickly. So once more, use your learner's natural ability to connect to make learning stick.

Do you believe that reading and underlining important data can help you learn and revise?

Sadly, that is untrue. You need to recall information repeatedly in order for your brain's neural networks to activate and form connections while you're attempting to learn anything. Reading fosters recognition and familiarity, which are misleading learning allies. You're better off taking your own notes or utilising mind maps to graphically represent important concepts. Now that you've dispelled a few common misconceptions regarding learning, let me share with you another fascinating development mindset truth. Education expert Carol Dweck demonstrates how our attitude toward learning is the key to our success. A growth mindset encourages flexible and active learning. They embrace criticism and learn from their errors. Fixed-minded people don't think they can change.

It is natural and has been successful for thousands of years to hang fresh knowledge onto existing hooks. Although the human species as a whole has comparable brain architecture, each individual will connect to their own unique linkages, and we need to make use of that. This is crucial for L&D since we frequently need to persuade individuals to acquire the same habits or information, potentially the same content. What can you then do to support individuals in making solid connections to the appropriate knowledge or tasks? It's simple to ask someone what they already know about X before teaching them something new when imparting information. Encourage them to pass along the links they already have to others.

Emotional memories are labelled by neurotransmitters as "This is significant". The trick to this one is paying attention. People are often bad eyewitnesses since they didn't pay attention and can't recall the specifics. Of course, repetition, repetition, repetition is what this is. Trainers occasionally make the error of doing the repetitions, but in order for learners to build their neural connections, they actually need to complete the repetitions. This thing is a novelty. We pay attention to new or unusual items because we don't yet know if they are safe or hazardous, thus we recall them. Regularly surprise your leraners, but don't scare them. This is an example of exercise, which is less common than it ought to be in traditional classroom settings or online learning.

However, a ton of studies demonstrates how closely our bodies and minds are intertwined, and exercise improves our ability huge learn. People need to remember what they just learned, not merely identify it, while reflecting. Recognition is a phoney ally. Although we have a sense of what we know or how to do something, we may not be able to recollect it. Finally, all of the concepts you just discussed are included in this element. Stories connect concepts, are compelling, emotive, and often repeated. They frequently also contain innovative aspects. Tell them while strolling or listen to them at the fitness centre. Good stories are also simple to remember and tell again. A pneumonic to help you recall a collection of linked or unrelated items is included as a supplementary learning tool. Use the learners pneumonic going forward to incorporate each component on this list when creating or presenting sticky training!

When you want to be more imaginative but are having problems, you can find it helpful to ask yourself, "What does an innovator's brain look like?" What exactly did they do to alter their minds in this manner? Let's examine two crucial brain areas that alter when you are inventive and how you might influence these changes. The frontopolar cortex comes first. I know how to turn this on, and it's right here in front of your brain. You need to apply analogical reasoning to activate this innovation-related portion of your brain. Simply put, this implies making analogies. Imagine you want to expand your reach and create a new marketing plan. Consider metaphors like the sun, which illuminates the entire planet; a news network with a large audience; or a real viral illness that spreads swiftly and contagiously. Each day, billions of individuals could be reached by all of these. similar to what you hope your marketing plan will accomplish. You must ask yourself, "What elements of these parallels can I use in my marketing plan?"

If you want to employ analogical thinking. Your frontopolar cortex will then start to perform its magic as your brain begins to form connections. You might wonder, if the sun is dependable, how can your business be more dependable? You may inquire as to how you could be more inclusive given that it is unequal. You might wonder whether you might create enough internal noise through open blogging so that the company's energy spreads broadly. It glows from within thanks to explosions on its surface. A news station is one example of a source that offers information about current events. Can your business also do this? Can you make updates to your website to establish yourself as a trustworthy source for the newest trends? Can you accurately identify danger? Can you occasionally entertain us with jokes and encouraging stories? You may link the pertinent and beneficial features of this to viral outbreaks.

You could wonder, for example, if we can naturally transmit a message by word of mouth, given that viral outbreaks can spread through contamination. What will spread the word quickly? What will render the message contagious but benign? What will ensure its durability? Simply posing these questions will stimulate the frontopolar cortex, which in turn will spark fresh creative thoughts. Your brain will work harder to come up with new ideas, the more obscure the analogy is. However, research suggests that it's ideal to make an unexpected but reasonable comparison.

According to research, there are three main characteristics shared by businesses that execute strategy more quickly than others. They are more united, more agile, and have better clarity. Let's examine how you might alter your thinking in order to alter your brain and operate more quickly and effectively. They sought to comprehend ways to alter their perspective in order for the group to launch their items more quickly. I started by considering clarity. I found that although the team looked to be highly driven and goal-oriented, they were unable to clearly recognise new options due to stress. That's because stress switches the brain into habit mode, which clouds fresh ideas. Next, we considered oneness. The design and programming teams worked separately, which prevented the company's teams from becoming cohesive. And although the programming staff was incredibly intelligent, we discovered that their obsessiveness made them less nimble.

Consequently, we went on to examine each component separately while applying the following findings from brain research: When stress causes the brain to become habituated, it hinders clarity. Unity is improved when the theory of mind area of the brain is activated. Agility is boosted when feedback control circuits in the brain are impacted. Naturally, you must put these insights into practise if you want to use them. Stress comes first. Make sure you aren't continuously checking in on your goals if you are anxious. Although having a goal in mind might be beneficial, it can also make you more stressed out by over-activating your brain's fight, flight, or free circuits. You won't be able to properly recognise new and essential adjustments as a result, which will reinforce old patterns.

According to studies, managers and other leaders would be better suited to showing compassion to their workers than making them always focus on their objectives. For example, emphasising someone's strengths may inspire them more. When compassion calms individuals, they are freed from the mental and behavioural patterns that stress causes, allowing them to think more clearly and generate fresh ideas. Then there is harmony. For this to happen, the team must be well coordinated. If you take into account all team members' perspectives, your chances of uniting the group are significantly improved.

It's important to enable other people's opinions to influence our own, in addition to just putting all viewpoints on the table. We might wonder why the other viewers are important rather than reacting to differences. For instance, highlighting someone's qualities could inspire them more. When compassion calms individuals, they are freed from the mental and behavioural patterns that stress causes, allowing them to think more clearly and generate fresh ideas. Then there is harmony. The team must be well coordinated for this to happen.

If you take into account all team members' perspectives, your chances of uniting the group are significantly improved. It's important to enable other people's opinions to influence our own, in addition to just putting all viewpoints on the table. We might wonder why the other viewers are important rather than reacting to differences. What might you learn if you approached the issue from a different angle? And it's not necessary to meet in person to achieve this. You may accomplish this by working online or through group messaging. We need to make use of the brain's rapid change and response capabilities if we want to be more agile.

There are various ways to accomplish this; however, let's focus on one in particular. Signal control is the capacity to differentiate between dramatic and pertinent feedback. Someone stating that your supervisor is unhappy might be dramatic feedback. Why bother scheduling a meeting if your boss is not there? If you are meeting with your supervisor and they are not feeling well, that would be pertinent input. Right now, you need to care. It helps your brain feel less overloaded when you break things down into relevant and dramatic pieces. So, as you can see, having clarity, unity, and agility can assist your brain function more quickly so that you can quickly implement a new approach. Start by asking yourself, what is most problematic in my team? Are they ambiguous? Not cohesive? Not enough agility? At your subsequent meeting, implement one of the aforementioned proposals.

What makes a team the smartest it can possibly be?

It is neither the team's average intellect nor the team member with the highest level of intelligence. When there is collective intelligence, a team is as intelligent as it possibly can be. But it might be difficult to access and articulate this intelligence. Continue reading to learn what collective intelligence is, why it matters, and how to improve it on your team.

Collective intelligence exceeds each team member's average IQ. You see, every person's brain, to a greater or lesser extent, is altered and impacted by the brains of other team members while they are there. Because you have a network in your brain that reflects other people's points of view as well, you may deduce what others are thinking when you experience their feelings. This network of brain cells is known as a "mirror neuron network. You could wonder if I share their emotions or if my team member's perspective differs from theirs. They wanted to know if customers would buy their new product, but they couldn't agree on how much information to give them ahead of time, for fear that competitors in the same market would learn about it first and move into the market faster. They were more concerned with entrepreneurs than with other large corporations.

I can only release the product and test it, thought one-half of the crew. The other half said that companies needed to build obstacles to prevent competitors from entering the market first. These divergent viewpoints and feelings can gradually permeate our brains and affect the way we think. However, if we think independently, we could merely act on our first instinct. Because you have a network in your brain that reflects other people's points of view as well, you may deduce what others are thinking when you experience their feelings. This network of brain cells is known as a "mirror neuron network". You could wonder if I share their emotions or if my team member's perspective differs from theirs.

I formerly worked for a Fortune 500 company's sales development division. They wanted to know if customers would buy their new product, but they couldn't agree on how much information to give them ahead of time, for fear that competitors in the same market would learn about it first and move into the market faster. They were more concerned with entrepreneurs than with other large corporations. I can only release the product and test it, thought one-half of the crew. The other half said that companies needed to build obstacles to prevent competitors from entering the market first. These divergent viewpoints and feelings can gradually permeate our brains and affect the way we think.

However, if we think independently, we could merely act on our first instinct. It's possible that the risk-averse group released the product too slowly. Additionally, the group that only wanted to test the goods may have regretted their sloppy behaviour. But as they discussed risk and urgency, each half saw the value in the other, and they came to a decision that included both points of view. They tested the product rapidly in the end, but they also safeguarded their algorithm, introduced features that would be difficult to imitate, and coordinated the efforts of the teams in charge of product development, sales, and marketing to hasten the final release. This is the appearance of improved collective intelligence.

There are three easy measures that may be taken to improve collective intelligence. First, compile the group's collective viewpoints. Then create persuasive reasons for your viewpoint. It is known as hypothesis. Finally, create strong arguments in support of the opposing viewpoints. The conflicting hypothesis 2 is the name of this additional compelling viewpoint. This kind of analysis, in which the first and second hypotheses contend with one another, is known as an analysis of competing hypotheses.

Prejudice can be avoided when you take into account both points of view. A region of the brain that is trained to understand others' points of view is activated when you attempt to guess what someone else is thinking. This boosts collective intelligence. Collective intelligence can exist without physical presence. Online development is another option. Keep in mind that there are frequently several alternative solutions available when presented with a difficult scenario. Talking about this may improve decision-making, innovation, and strategy, as well as collective intelligence.

Your brain is directly impacted by this, and you may take specific actions to better handle these difficulties. I'll explain to you what fear and worry do to the brain and how you and your group can counteract this by rewiring your neural pathways. At one point, I was a part of a high-potential team for a high-end medical instrument manufacturing company. The team's branding and marketing strategy have undergone a significant transformation. The following generation of leaders was thus extremely nervous and scared that they wouldn't be able to guide their employees to successfully market the revised brand. They wanted to know how I might ease their dread and anxiety so they could feel more resilient in the face of the enormous unknowns that lay ahead of them. I explained that when we experience such worries, the amygdala, our brain's emotion processor, is active, and because the amygdala is related to the brain's primary cognitive circuits, those circuits also experience overload. The secret is to reduce amygdala blood flow so that your thinking brain is less overworked. By doing this, you can analyse risks, innovate, and make better judgments.

As you can see, your brain tends to overreact in times of anxiety. It is thought that negative things will continue indefinitely. Use self-talk to remind yourself that this too shall pass as a reality check. Your brain will respond with greater efficiency when you say this. Check for stability of mind . We frequently worry about uncontrollable factors. Decide on two or three things that are beyond your control, then choose to let them go and check your ability . Your brain will have more room to think as a result. Also known as a focus shift, this is the constant focus on the solution rather than the problem. This has five implications for the high potential squad I coached for a premium brand. They would first divide their plan into quarterly intervals. That is a lump. When they were nervous, they would practise mindfulness by blocking out their thoughts. Afterward, they would give themselves and their employees a reality check by reminding them that the anxiety over the new plan would soon pass. They would also quit worrying excessively about things like the stock market and control checks that were beyond their control. And lastly, when they encountered problems, they would exchange ideas for solutions, shifting their focus.

Do you know that mindfulness can improve your decision-making, sleep, and even alter your genes to lengthen your life?

Regular usage of mindfulness in this manner will transform your brain from an overloaded state to a problem-solving powerhouse. You've probably heard that practising mindfulness may make you feel more at ease. Let's examine what mindfulness is, how it affects the brain, and the many methods for practising it. Simply focusing all of your attention on the current moment is mindfulness. Whatever mental chitchat is going on, you ignore it. You don't care about the past, other people's diversions, or your anxieties about the future. You just maintain open awareness and judgment-free presence in the here and now.

Of course, it's difficult to focus on one thing, and you may occasionally lose focus. But if it happens, just return to the current time. Mindfulness causes your brain to become a lot calmer. Additionally, you are able to think more clearly, which makes it simpler and less taxing to make judgments. You are also less prone to distractions while you are in this mental state. There are many different ways that you may practise mindfulness. The simplest method is to close your eyes, focus like a spotlight on your breath, and hold that focus. Bring the flashlight back to your breath if it starts to move. Start with five minutes, then gradually extend it to twenty. You may also practise walking meditation if being motionless is not your thing. But if it happens, just return to the current time.

Mindfulness causes your brain to become lot calmer. Additionally, you are able to think more clearly, which makes it simpler and less taxing to make judgments. You are also less prone to distractions while you are in this mental state. There are many different methods that you may practise mindfulness. The simplest method is to close your eyes, focus like a spotlight on your breath, and hold that focus. Bring the flashlight back to your breath if it starts to move. Start with five minutes, then gradually extend it to twenty. You may also practise walking meditation if being motionless is not your thing. On your commute to work, you may put this into practise.

On your drive to work or coming home, you may put this into practise. Alternately, schedule it during your lunch hour. Find a calm area where you may walk carefully and slowly to practise this. First, remain still and observe your surroundings. Next, focus on your firmly planted feet to remind yourself of your connection to the earth.

There are a few stages to talk through in order to control this mental turbulence. First, identify the emotional cost of change that you must bear. This is the changeover cost. If you desire effective change, you must pay with emotions in a same way that you would if you were purchasing a new laptop. According to research, using this strategy increases your brain's commitment to change. Draw two columns, labelled column A and column B, to begin. You list all of the benefits of your current selection in column A. You can remark, for instance, that I need to make time to learn a new platform. You list all of the benefits of the new option in column B. For instance, you may claim that using this platform will save me time. Your chances of feeling the shift as more bearable increase as your brain becomes more adept at distinguishing between columns B and A.

The spread of options is shown by the appeal between the contrasts in columns A and B. Your brain will be more inclined to go forward the more it takes in the variations or dispersion between the two columns. You must be careful to be genuine and acknowledge the benefits. You will relate better to statements such, "I will have more time for my kids or I will have more time to myself," than "I will save time." Build column B till your mind is persuaded. There is a cost associated with change, as you can see, but if your brain accepts that the cost is justified, change will be that much simpler.

You may demonstrate to the rest of the business why you lack a magic training wand and why you can't simply bombard them with additional information and expect success using quantifiable statistics and science. With quantifiable facts and science, you can demonstrate to the rest of the company why there isn't a magic training wand and why you can't just slam people with more information and expect it to stick, but you can show them how you can aid in the transition from learning to performance. Despite the fact that your brain is actually pink, neuroscience offers us the authority to demonstrate that learning isn't light and fluffy. Because the finest brain trick is asking questions. Your brain nearly always links new information with old, as appropriate networks are activated to link the new input and make it more memorable.

Positive emotions are less infectious than negative ones, such as fear and wrath. You might be curious as to why it's simpler to transmit irrational emotions like fear than irrational emotions like enthusiasm. This, according to researchers, occurs for evolutionary reasons. Our minds are built to seek safety. Fear and fury are the first emotions that our brains process because they are designed to protect us above all else. Fear and fury are the first emotions that our brains process because they are designed to protect us above all else.

Mirror neurons are incredibly beneficial when you want to understand how someone else feels, such as when they're upset because they lost a loved one, but you have to make certain changes, or, to put it another way, throw a towel over the mirror when you don't want to experience what they're experiencing. I refer to these as countermirroring methods. Understanding how to do this may be quite beneficial at work. By doing three things, you can avoid having your own mood ruined by someone else's bad mood by doing three things. You might also enter their office and make a commendable statement, such as "Great report last week," for example. I can't cope with you, you might be tempted to say, but you won't because your focus will be on the good. Another tactic is to just continue talking about the current problem while gazing away at something pleasant in your coworker's office. Such a lovely picture. This straightforward advice will shield you from other people's disruptive, infectious emotions at work.

Have you ever wondered why you've never had the courage to ask for that promotion, submit an application for a position at a better organisation, or start that start-up that you know would be a wonderful idea?

You know those days when you get into work in a terrific mood but the person sitting next to you isn't? Before you know it, you're feeling down as well. That must be frustrating. The reason their mood affects you is that it's biologically based that emotions are contagious. Let's talk about the scientific reasons for infectious emotions and what you can do if someone else's mood affects your own. Right, if I were joyful, my brain's happiness circuits would be active, and if I passed a colleague who was upset, their brain's anger circuits would be active. Until now, so good? The tale doesn't end here, which is great. We don't simply have our own feelings in our brains while we're among other people. We physically bear their feelings as well. This is so because our brains include groups of nerve cells called mirror neurons, which are programmed to reflect other people's emotions. Because of their stronger basic empathy, certain people are more sensitive to the emotions of others. The greater your capacity for empathy, the better competent you will be to convey the other person's feelings.

Manipulation is a natural component of human life. It has existed and will continue to exist forever. By learning the strategies and tricks, you can either use them effectively yourself or defend yourself against those who might use them against you. The information is right in front of you. Simply extend your hand and accept it. Being manipulated is not always a terrible thing. In particular, I'll look at how to utilise manipulation to achieve goals that pave the road to a great life and a lifetime of achievement. I'll look at techniques for rewiring the brain to get rid of harmful negative beliefs that get in the way of achieving success. Neuro-Linguistic Programming must be discussed in any discussion of mind control and manipulation. NLP is a technique used by many experts and laypeople to teach people how to correctly train their minds in order to create and achieve their personal goals.

Manipulation strategy imparts the useful abilities employed by exceptional communicators. The foundation for producing good results is effective communication. For professional competence in counselling, education, and business, NLP abilities are proven to be beneficial. Do you think it's possible to manipulate the human mind? For a very long time, many individuals have found the subject of mind control to be interesting.

Though it sometimes gets a bad name, manipulation is actually just the study of human cognitive processes and actions. Perhaps as a manager, you're having trouble persuading your employees to pay attention to you. Perhaps you are dealing with a manipulator in your life and would like to discover new approaches to handle them or counteract their tactics. Maybe you're just interested in the idea and want to know how people can be controlled.

Why should employees work harder?

Employees in businesses need to completely understand why they are employed by the company. Yet, this is frequently not the case. It has an impact on their conduct and output. For instance, how does the Apple company succeed? That is why they have devoted employees. What compelled them to work for the organisation? Definitely, it is not simply due to money. It has to do with how Apple inspires people to work for the organisation.

In NLP philosophy, active listening is another talent. An employee who actively listens performs better at work. How does language facilitate improved communication among employees? Communication involves more than simply giving facts; it also involves communicating opinions and feelings. As a result, NLP pioneers discovered a few traits that successful people shared. Their speech, particularly the terms they use, what sort of inquiry , their voices' pitch, their physical postures and gestures (essentially, body language) (basically, body language), their ability to listening. Therefore, NLP theory is effective in inspiring workers to boost their output and communication.

If you examine this closely, you will see that many people generally lack these basic communication skills. These abilities are not as valued by many as academics. because of the widespread perception that academic achievement is more important than anything else. According to them, behavioural patterns are less important than study patterns. Yes, it is crucial, but communication skills also have a significant influence on academic abilities. If you observe a smart employee with excellent academic knowledge but poor communication skills, an employee with excellent communication skills and average knowledge will succeed over the other. Communication can occasionally alter a person's viewpoint, thoughts, or beliefs. This is referred to as mental programming. This may have an impact on a person's brain's language. Therefore, we may conclude that NLP is a programme that modifies a person's brain through influencing his thinking by altering his language and behavioural patterns.

One of the most effective methods to read people is through their body language. Humans are predisposed to move their bodies in a particular way in response to their emotions and conscious as well as subconscious thoughts. Understanding body language clues will advance your analytical abilities and enhance your ability to interact with others in all facets of life.

Your résumé, cover letter, and interview techniques can all be significantly improved by NLP. This complete strategy helps us overcome the barriers in our brains to accomplish our goals and is beneficial in both our professional and personal lives. Science now understands how the brain works and controls our thoughts, words, and deeds. We may then modify this to accomplish our objectives. We can also modify a habit, manage our emotions, or even get rid of a phobia.

We can modify our ideas in order to feel better at work. As a result of evolution, we tend to focus on our negative ideas. NLP pushes us to reframe this perspective in order to generate ebullient ideas. Additionally, it reminds us that everything that occurs is neutral and that we have control over our thoughts. For instance, even though you enjoy writing out your weekly report since it clarifies your thoughts and demonstrates how much you have accomplished, a coworker could find it tedious and difficult to execute. Writing the report prompts two utterly different responses to the identical job. Therefore, by altering the way we think about the tasks we find challenging, we may also alter the feelings we associate with them and, as a result, significantly lessen the aggravation we experience at work. Here are some warm-up activities for you.

Your body language can be used in place of words. It provides immediate feedback. Because body language explains words through gestures and postures, a worker with excellent body language can work considerably more effectively. The employee will be less affected by language if they are a passive listener because they will be less engaged. These five factors—beliefs, values, frames of reference, questions, and emotional states—taken together might motivate us to act or keep us immobile. This technique was developed via analysis and comprehension of the relationship between how "neuro" (nerve) communication functions, how language is impacted, and how human behaviour is altered.

Use of positive vs negative language. If you just take away one lesson from NLP, it's that we construct our world. And since our ideas determine the way we speak, our thoughts also influence how we see the outside world. Tony Robbins suggests utilising transformational vocabulary because of this. Tony Robbins said, "Words shape our beliefs, which in turn influence our behaviors." Make a list of the unfavourable terms you employ and try to replace them with ones that are Your thinking will start to shift as a result It's a challenge instead of "It's impossible." "I know nothing" changes to "I learn something new every day."

Constantly shifting viewpoints clarifying your views is the crucial next step after using encouraging language. Sometimes all it takes to turn a situation around is to change your perspective—at work, for instance. In his lectures, Tony Robbins shows that it is possible to get over any constrained mindset. Participants even run over hot coals as part of a mind-over-matter activity at the conclusion of their events. We may strive to banish the negative beliefs that limit our potential and make us feel awful without ever going to that extreme. Make a note of the phrases that come to mind when you think of bad situations, and then change each one into a positive notion that you will think of each time the unpleasant event arises. Yes, it is a conscious effort.

Emotional Examination It's in our inclination to hold others accountable for our mistakes or disappointments. Does that make you think of anything? Examine your schedule and documents to check if they are as organised as you believe. As an exercise, write down all of your concerns about a coworker who irritates you. Point out the shortcomings they possess that you are aware of in yourself, and then remedy them. Even though it may seem strange, we frequently become annoyed by things in others that make us feel bad about ourselves. Our irritation with others will disappear after we address these problems in ourselves, and the relationship will only improve.

Preventing resentment with a bucket list The effects of jealousy on our working relationships are negative. How can we respond more effectively to things like more pay, higher-level tasks, and longer vacations to prevent envy and sustain harmonious relationships? We may use it as a means to examine ourselves if we realise we are envious of our coworkers. Write out what that person has accomplished that you would aspire to do yourself one day if jealously arises. Afterward, start thinking about when and how you can make it happen. Naturally, you should also remember to smile for your coworker because they would do the same for you. Congratulate them on their impending international business trip, their 20% pay increase, or their planned appearance at a prestigious conference.

We must choose to believe in one another. However, in order to succeed professionally, you must also make the commitment to being your own best friend and maintaining the commitments you made to yourself. Exercise: Pay attention to the time required for your commitment to work for one week: Get a good night's sleep to prepare for a productive day at work, devote a certain amount of time to a personal goal, and so on.

Getting Hired

Building rapport through matching job criteria with phrases from a job description, an advertisement, or business expectations is known as matching and mirroring. You'll be relieved to learn that this is nothing new; for more than a decade, CV writers have been honing the skill of creating engrossing, subconscious, motivating, and intriguing material for CVs and resumes. There are several psychological techniques you can use to make your CV or resume more effective, such as drawing attention to the areas you want recruiters to focus on and how you can make it stand out.

Achievements, ROI, or influence on the CV help us hold the reader's interest for longer and arouse curiosity. By emphasising promotions, advancements, or transfers on your CV or resume and then bringing readers back to your accomplishments, ROI, and influence, we create an anticipation loop and pique interest in further reading. We start with a fascinating and succinct explanation of your skill or obligations. The market and the hiring manager's perspective must be known and understood before producing any CV or resume, because that is where most of the writing originates. Considering the language you wish to use, that will have the biggest influence on your profile. It might provide you with the best opportunity to bargain for a better income. Remember that even if you have a strong CV or resume, you won't get the job until you can mirror and match it in the interview and learn to add NLP psychological factors that will allow you to start bargaining for the wage you desire.

Stay focused on the goal you want to achieve. The idea that certain people have more "luck" than others and that success is simpler for them is conveyed by statements like "He is blessed" or "He has a golden touch." "Luck" does not exist in NLP. In Unlimited Power, Robbins states that "your actions, and not your circumstances, define your future." He repeatedly demonstrates how successful people set objectives and take all the necessary steps to achieve them. We get the idea that it was fortunate to have that goal and be alone with it. " Extraordinary lives are not reserved for the fortunate few. As human beings, it is our birthright. It is available for your use. You must focus on a goal and seize every chance that presents itself to accomplish it each day if you want to attain it.

Make a list of all the easy tasks that can help you achieve your goal, and then map out the steps you need to take to get there. Congratulate yourself on completing each stage, then focus on the one after that. Because it keeps us motivated, NLP is a very effective technique to help us advance in our jobs. It's a valuable toolset for managers because it enables them to comprehend their employees, to show consideration, and to manage them more effectively. Employees benefit from it by learning new skills, stepping outside of their comfort zones to advance professionally, improving their skills, or even landing a better job, according to Jeanneau. Even more so, in his opinion, NLP need to be taught in schools since it "would enable each of us establish effortless, deeper, more harmonious connections with others and ourselves."However, since positively using our minds is an exercise, we need to do it every day for it to be effective. And the second difficulty is that this is a personal road that no one can pursue for you, as you have undoubtedly already realised.

> *Are you prepared to perform these workouts in order to enhance your personal and professional lives?*

Abandoning judgement It is more effective than mirroring emotions to completely let go of making judgments about other people, as encouraged by NLP. The terrible urge to judge does not help us and may perhaps be detrimental. Not only does it not improve your coworker's conduct and won't because you won't tell her, but it may also make you feel awful, insecure, and even furious. In practise, you can stop yourself from passing judgement and consciously change the thinking that is causing it. The more you do this, the more natural it will become.

> *"Last but not least, the NLP model aids workers in fostering trust, gaining a clear understanding of their objectives, boosting productivity, helping others, improving communication, understanding other people's perspectives, and developing their personalities and leadership abilities."- Dr. Amit Das*

CHAPTER FOUR

Transforming Organisation Through NLP

"Pessimistic thoughts will only yield trees unwilling to bear edible fruit. Optimistic thinking will always feed those who are willing to sit at your table"."— Michaelson Williams

Connection between NLP and its use in the human resources field.

Everyone now realises that in order to achieve commercial greatness, an organisation must hire the greatest talent and work hard to keep it. NLP can handle a variety of tasks inside an organisational structure. Human interactions at work are a critical area for any HR professional in an organisational setting. The outside environment in which workers work has a significant influence on how they view their employment. Along with the external environment, the internal environment within the employee is equally vital for productivity. The words we say to ourselves have a big impact on the internal environment we construct for ourselves.

Our thoughts, beliefs, attitudes, assumptions, and emotions all contribute to this environment. For instance, a team member could feel insecure if the team leader and employee have a poor working relationship. This nervousness might lead to the team being too controlled. The team spirit will be ruined as a result. The key HR process, including hiring, training delivery, communication channels, negotiating, customer service, and stress management, is where NLP has a significant impact on the organisation.

> "*According to research, the following are the areas where NLP has the biggest impact:The ability to respond to criticism is improved through the calibration of non-verbal cues, outcome-based thinking, rapport building, understanding of thinking styles, motivational values through metaprograms, flexibility in communication, leadership, persuasion, training delivery, and content curation.*"

Let's investigate the connection between NLP and its use in the human resources field. Any organisation's human resources are one of its most valuable resources. A procedure of utmost importance is the hiring and selection of smart, talented workers in order to develop a durable competitive edge. According to Beck and Walmsley (2012), hiring a bright and skilled individual gives the company an advantage over its rivals.

- According to NLP, a person is a whole mind-body system. The entire mind-body system of an individual arrives at work each day. This system has its own thought and reaction patterns.
- According to NLP, a person's subjective experience is stored in three different representational systems. According to NLP, a person's subjective experience is represented in three different representational systems: visual (V), auditory (A), and kinesthetic (K).
- NLP is a popular and frequently used instrument for interpersonal growth and communication. Professionals, including teachers, managers, trainers, salesmen, market researchers, counsellors, consultants, and attorneys, use it all over the world . NLP has been effectively used in the following fields by individuals all around the world: Education, training, and development; coaching; personal growth; family counseling; management auditing; advertising; sales; and human resources.

The idea of the use of neurolinguistic programming in human resources has been researched and evaluated, and factual data, conclusions, and results have been published in several research articles. According to the study and conclusions, NLP is extremely useful for recruiting in human resources. Business owners and other professionals of today are always considering how to get a competitive edge in the current environment of fast change and technological innovation. Numerous HR and business professionals are aware of the benefits that NLP may provide for various industries.

"Professionals in the fields of human resources, learning and development, training, recruiting, organisational development, reward, and employee relations are constantly on the lookout for learning opportunities that will improve their abilities as communicators, coaches, mentors, time managers, talent scouts, managers of change, and people developers."

All human resource managers and leaders have the desire to learn more about and assist other associates so they can develop and be the greatest versions of themselves (and we're all looking for methods to generate better outcomes, so this is something we all strive to do). The study of what separates the outstanding from the average has been dubbed the art and science of personal excellence, or NLP (Neuro Linguistic Programming). The terms "neuro" and "linguistic" refer to how our minds work, respectively, while "programming" refers to our thought and behaviour patterns. It has been referred to as "practical behavioural psychology" by some. It examines how humans assimilate and analyse data from the environment.

Let's face it, business is essentially about interactions between two people at its most fundamental level. Therefore, how well they can engage, communicate, and process information is crucial to success. The foundation of all communication is rapport, which is also crucial for effective relationship-building, coaching, and influence.

NLP examines behaviour patterns to see if they are beneficial and provide the intended results; if not, we may make changes to increase success. It is a tool for exemplifying greatness, reproducing it within ourselves, and sharing it with others. I'm now working with a retailer that is using NLP to enhance customer service, boost sales, and help executives better understand, teach, and communicate with their team members. They have seen an increase in average customer spending of $30 as a result (so the ROI on the training they delivered is fantastic). There are sceptics, of course; they stress the dearth of data supporting the effectiveness of NLP. This debate often makes me think of the medical community, which for years said there was no evidence that eating fruits and vegetables may lower your risk of developing cancer and heart disease.

We are all advised to consume a lot of fruit and vegetables now that it is a reality that has been well investigated and verified. Simply said, science is still lagging behind (a good example of this is the NLP technique of anchoring—science has now proved how it works). It is possible to get the "evidence" that some people are looking for by speaking with individuals and organisations that have used NLP to boost achievement, alter outcomes, and bring about transformation: NLP has evolved since the 1970s, but its emphasis on practical application has not changed. The NLP community at that time was never preoccupied with showing that what they did worked (learning and teaching what works and gets results). Simply said, science is still lagging behind (a good example of this is the NLP technique of anchoring — science has now proved how it works).

It is possible to get the "evidence" that some people are looking for by speaking with individuals and organisations that have used NLP to boost achievement, alter outcomes, and bring about transformation: If I could suggest one course to my management and HR peers, it would be an NLP practitioner course. I'm continuously in awe of the transformations you can effect in others, enabling them to reach their full potential. I believe that NLP's overarching attitude is what has helped me the most. One of the most important lessons I've learned is that you have choices and are accountable for them. The NLP models are helpful in creating training programmes, coaching and mentoring team members, getting ready for meetings and presentations, and developing rapport with stakeholders for improved interactions.

Having worked in HR , I am aware of the pressure many of my colleagues face to find the "solution" and advise business executives on how to solve people issues and assist employees in meeting and exceeding company targets and goals. Like many departments, their task is to do more with fewer employees. As professionals, we want tools that are simple to understand and use to help us get the results we want personally, as well as tools we can share with businesses to help them.

> *"Anything that improves our communication, influence, relationship-building, relationship-building, presentation, and coaching skills is extremely valuable and increases our effectiveness."*

Here are a few instances showing how NLP may benefit colleagues in HR & Training:

- Communication and persuasion NLP shows us how to develop rapport with anyone. We can build connections of deep trust and get along with everyone thanks to our rapport-building abilities. It allows us to exert even more influence on others we may not directly control. Knowing how others perceive the world and how they like to process it might help us communicate with them in a way that suits them, for example, by using predicates. A few well worded questions may drastically save time, thus improved listening and questioning abilities are essential and very important to all of us.

- The way that successful people define their goals determines how effective they are. Learn how to develop detailed, motivating goals that will help people achieve anything they desire in life and in their jobs. Precise inquiries How to pose key questions in HR scenarios that get directly to the point.

- Have a toolbox of techniques and methods of thinking that may assist your customers in overcoming challenges and better understanding their teams and themselves. Traditional coaching encourages individuals to think creatively about their issues, but NLP skills provide you enhanced listening and questioning techniques that make you far more effective.

- Using NLP, hone your chairing abilities. Learn how to read your group with calibration skills and sensory acuity, provide them information in a style that best suits them (visual, aural, or kinesthetic), and master the art of gracefully handling problems.

- Develop the flexibility to speak in "big picture" terms and to dig down into the details as necessary.

- Learn to bargain effectively to prevent conflict and consistently produce win-win results.

- Learn how to arrange presentations such that they will hold the attention of the whole audience, how to utilise metaphors or storytelling that engages (and educates), how to employ internally recognised gestures to support your message, and how to move (or not move) on stage to facilitate delivery.

- Computers exchange information using binary code, which consists solely of zeros and ones. It takes sophisticated technological advancement to go from bits and bytes to conversational English—or any other human language.

As HR professionals, we frequently neglect to offer ourselves opportunity to learn and improve. We all have things that personally hold us back, whether they be self-limiting ideas, internal conflicts, nervousness in a certain situation, or memories of the past that hold us back - the list is endless. The NLP practitioner training gives us the tools we need to overcome obstacles, create realistic goals for ourselves, and connect our motivation to our objectives. It's taken a while, but natural language processing, or NLP, in artificial intelligence (AI), has now developed to the point where applications can substitute for human agents in a variety of ways, many of which are appearing in eLearning and performance support systems.

There are a few examples of how L&D teams are already utilising NLP in E-Learning in this post, but it is by no means an exhaustive list. NLP technologies use algorithms to recognise speech constituents, examine grammar, and determine the purpose of each word in a phrase or sentence. They can then interpret comments or requests and give the proper response. In order to "learn" to execute tasks that people generally accomplish, such as voice recognition, learning speech patterns and variations, and constructing answers that resemble human conversation, NLP depends on other fields of AI, such as machine learning and deep learning. These tools enable NLP-powered apps to operate freely and without being constrained by a predefined set of replies. The Future Today Institute refers to this next era of computing as "cognitive computing," where computers reason and solve problems, as being brought about by the ability of AI-powered technology to learn from experience and inputs.

When utilising an NLP-based technology, a user may write, speak, or otherwise input text to the app or device: A learner uses NLP when he asks Siri a question, tells him smart speaker to play music, or dictates a text or email. As an alternative, a student might use a messaging or email app, where an NLP-powered function might offer word completions.

NLP is also used by email applications that offer suggestions for replies to incoming messages. Depending on the context in which a term is used, it might mean something entirely different in numerous languages. The creation of NLP algorithms was extremely challenging due to this "structural ambiguity." The online game, in which players try to stump the computer, demonstrates and explains how one NLP algorithm handles structural ambiguity by "learning" all of a word's potential meanings before examining the other words in a phrase to determine the word's precise meaning in a given context. E-Learning NLP Because of how frequently natural language processing is used in E-Learning, learners might not be aware of this fact due to the technology's widespread integration into apps and platforms.

First-line customer service or technical assistance is provided, including responses to routine, common questions and the escalation of more difficult issues to a human agent. Help new workers through the onboarding process by providing them with information or links to forms, notifying them of tasks they need to do, and reminding them of deadlines. Between in-person or online class sessions, mentors by reviewing the information presented or posing exam questions. Check in with the students and invite them to consider any new skills or observations they have made. Offer performance support by responding to inquiries, connecting staff to information or documents, aiding with simple tasks, or guiding them through infrequently used procedures. Offer spaced practise and drills to augment or reinforce face-to-face training or E-Learning.

Virtual assistants with voice capabilities are not just limited to chatbots for mobile devices. According to reports, more than 50 million American people utilise smart gadgets to complete everyday office activities. In certain businesses, voice-activated assistants may do things like link participants to conference calls and plan them. Apps with NLP capabilities can both produce and interpret text.

NLP may be applied to L&D to: Create quick content based on keywords to simplify the generation of content. Identifying relevant eLearning to offer to learners, classifying information, enabling searches, and extracting keywords from already existing content Determine the main topics or ideas in lengthy texts to summarise, helping to chunk lengthy content and tailor it to learners. Determine if a paragraph, such a comment on an E-Learning "smile sheet," conveys a positive or negative attitude to get a sense of how well-received E-Learning is among learners. To categorise, organise, and target material, look for patterns or themes in various texts. Allow cross-language communication and document exchange among staff members of international organisations by translating between languages. Make branching scenarios in E-Learning more lively and interesting by animating virtual trainers. Make voice-activated performance support tools so that workers may ask for help with the process.

How can you use emotions to make learning more memorable?

Emotions motivate and stick. Think about how you are feeling right now, and then quickly write it down or make an emoji. I drew a smiling yet focused expression because even while I'm having fun making this movie for you, I'm also paying attention to do it properly. Do you believe that your present feeling will hinder or facilitate learning? Keep an eye out, we'll be returning to this soon. Take a peek at this image right now. To gaze at it, did you cock your head? What do you think? Your head tilts in the same way you do when you're intrigued. Because your brain and body are fully intertwined, when your brain receives the signal "tilted head," it correlates it with inquiry.

You start to feel true curiosity. It's nearly hard to avoid learning when one has an exploratory attitude since curiosity drives inquiries and research. A rush of dopamine is also released when your curiosity is satiated, making you feel good and wanting to repeat the learning process. Use slanted graphics on flyers or slides to instantly pique interest. Your head tilts in the same way you do when you're intrigued. You start to feel true curiosity. It's nearly hard to avoid learning when one has an exploratory attitude since curiosity drives inquiries and research.

Which of your life's most memorable moments stands out the most?

You must incorporate emotional sticky notes if you want people to remember what they learn and act differently. The following is a list of emotions that may facilitate or obstruct learning. To determine whether you are now in a fantastic state for learning, compare your emoji to the ones on this list. Although people aren't always in the correct frame of mind to learn and you can't control another person's emotions, you can still have an impact on them via your planning and delivery.

I guess that most of them caused you to experience some sort of positive or negative emotion. Because they have developed to keep us secure and assure our survival, emotions are sticky. In essence, we recall things we wish to repeat or learn to avoid. Learn this by using emotions as sticky notes. At work, we need employees to put their new knowledge to use, and emotions are a catalyst for recall, judgement, and action. People who have damage to their amygdala, one of the brain's emotional regions, are unable to sense emotions and have trouble remembering things and making decisions. They are able to analyse an issue logically, yet they lack the motivation to act. Here are a few simple techniques for starting to tap into various emotional states.

- You can include some into your workout and some you can perform on the spot.
- Create riddles or puzzles to pique interest.
- Reduce tension by quickly doing breathing exercises.
- To keep people focused, often change things up and get them moving.
- Create tasks that are difficult but doable to encourage perseverance.
- Develop empathy by working in small groups.
- Plan activities during calm periods to encourage reflection and memory consolidation.
- Increase emotional connections by connecting learning to real-world scenarios, especially for supposedly dry

subjects. There is just dry training, in my opinion; there is no such thing as a dry topic. In order to make your instruction more memorable, make sure it is organically emotional.

Your brain requires a lot of energy, and processing dry, abstract knowledge is extremely taxing on it, so it becomes tired quickly. More information cannot be forced into it to make it stick. No new connections, networks, or firing will occur in your neurons. With information overload, all that happens is that you put forth extra effort to create or distribute knowledge that no one can comprehend. More information cannot be forced into it to make it stick. No new connections, networks, or firing will occur in your neurons. With information overload, all that happens is that you put forth extra effort to create or distribute knowledge that no one can comprehend. Time, money, and effort are all being wasted horribly.

Furthermore, it could even be harmful for compliance because avoiding danger isn't made easier by providing more information. Information needs to be organised so that people may consume it in manageable, linked pieces. That doesn't entail producing a tonne of microlearning, since that would merely add to the already excessive amount of knowledge. Attempt to compare it to eating out. It's better when you're hungry and have a need for food, to start with. You leave feeling filled yet unsatisfied nutritionally. In contrast, a gourmet lunch will walk you through your selections with a well-organised menu. You could decide that since you don't have time for dessert, you'll only have the starter and the entrée. The chef will have figured out how to pair the greatest flavours, connect the courses, and serve the food to you in the most enjoyable sequence.

Even though a gourmet dinner may have many components, you end up feeling full, fed, and eager to have another one thanks to smaller quantities, more variety, and time to digest between courses. Learn to cook by following a set meal, eating chunked yet linked portions, and taking some time to digest before continuing.

NLP is used by HR managers as soon as they begin the talent acquisition process. A member of HR asked me how neurolinguistic programming (NLP) can help HR managers. NLP may be used across the whole hiring process. The top five qualities that recruiters will demand in the upcoming year, according to a poll performed by many agencies, are: sales skills, communication skills, patience and flexibility, result-orientedness, and relationship-building abilities. You can succeed in these top five talents and many more with the help of neurolinguistic programming. NLP is the art and science of having a compelling end goal and adopting an action-oriented mindset up until you reach it. If you work in recruiting, treat yourself by acquiring practical skills. We had a protracted conversation, and the HR staff became enthusiastic about using NLP to help individuals perform at their best.

Today, I'll look at methods to reduce information overload so that your don't become overwhelmed and give up. NLP is employed to assist individuals in bettering themselves individually by fostering capacities like self-reflection, confidence, and communication. Figuring out what each person's deepest values are and how they influence their profession. Even if a candidate has exceptional talent, if their beliefs do not align with those of the company, they will damage the department's or organisation's culture. These individuals only notice the flaws in the anticipated new transformation.to determine their life's purpose or goal and how it relates to the business that is hiring them. A shared vision has a distinct advantage over others. HR Managers may access candidates' world maps using Meta Model inquiry in order to comprehend their skills, limiting beliefs, etc. Setting goals utilising effective well-formed outcomes, checking each employee's status on a regular basis with the wheel of life, and working toward even better outcomes from there.

In a world that moves quickly, deadlines are a constant. The employee's direct boss may shift gears to coaching with compliance, which lowers employee motivation and leads to more delays or products of poor quality. When Meta Programs are used, the direct supervisors may be given access to the employee's ticking time bombs and can be trained by HR to switch their coaching approach from compliance to compassion. Since 80% of the everyday work in most firms is boring, it is crucial to keep employees motivated to give their best efforts. HR managers might employ Meta Programs to find out what makes a person tick or drives them to perform at their best, HR managers might employ Meta Programs. There are several times during the term when the employee enters a shell or survival mode and loses confidence. The employee may be helped by the NLP tools and strategies used by the HR professionals to solve the issue or problem.

NLP is highly effective in resolving conflicts and merging the two sections that are apart since organisations do have disputes between workers and diverse roles in the interest of the organisation as a whole. Another useful technique in this situation is perceptual positioning. In order to create a win-win situation, it is important to understand the techniques utilised to produce both good and negative results.

Nowadays, automation and innovation are highly prevalent, and brainstorming sessions are widespread in all organisations at all levels of the hierarchical structure. Most of the time, meetings with diverse perspectives cannot be effective since they include dreamers, realists, and critics all at once. The Walt-Disney technique may be applied, and a better result is guaranteed. Storytelling and metaphors are quite effective in making recommendations to the subconscious.

We could go on and on about the lovely products that NLP has to offer for every aspect of life. NLP provides advantages for people from many walks of life. NLP is a User Manual for someone to lead a great life. Not just HR, but all those team leads, people in general, and even NLP hopefuls, might find this post helpful.

"Organisations must quickly adapt their working methods due to the rapid changes in technology and the shifting demands of the market, which may or may not be accepted by the employees since they must step outside of their comfort zone. NLP practitioners must step forward and shift their focus from the problem to the solution that the company is anticipating with the new transition. In the company, there aren't many role models, and HR would like to see more of them. NLP modelling may be used to simulate these high achievers." -Dr. Amit Das

References

- *NLP Secrets: Using NLP Techniques to Reprogram Yourself & Others Paperback – Import, 28 May 2020 by Nadine Watson.*
- *The Life Transforming power of NLP: Your true power lies within your mind. Nothing is impossible Paperback – 1 January 2018 by Manoj Keshav.*
- *The Ultimate Introduction to NLP: How to build a successful life Paperback – 3 January 2013 by Richard Bandler (Author), Alessio Roberti (Author), Owen Fitzpatrick.*
- *NLP: The Essential Guide to Neuro-Linguistic Programming Kindle Edition*
- *by NLP Comprehensive (Author), Tom Dotz (Author), Tom Hoobyar (Author), Susan Sanders (Author), 12 Feb, 2013.*
- *How to Take Charge of Your Life: The User's Guide to NLP Paperback – 2 January 2014 by Richard Bandler (Author), Owen Fitzpatrick (Author), Alessio Roberti.*
- *The Power of Your Subconscious Mind (Hardcover) – 1 December 2019 by Dr. Joseph Murphy (Author).*
- *Learning NLP Through Self-Coaching: Understand, learn and develop neurolinguistic programming with powerful NLP techniques - easily explained with exercises and examples Paperback – Import, 24 June 2019 by Paul Edelmaier.*
- *NLP Self Mastery: 12 Book Mega Bundle (Neuro-Linguistic Programming, Memory Improvement, Influence, Success 1) Kindle Edition by Modern Psychology Publishing.*

- *NLP Techniques: Using Neuro-Linguistic Programming to Transform Your Life Kindle Edition by Robyn Bell (Author), 12 July, 2022.*
- *The Big Book of NLP, Expanded: 350+ Techniques, Patterns & Strategies of Neuro Linguistic Programming: 6 (Nlp Neuro Linguistic Programming) Paperback – 2 August 2010 by Marina Schwarts (Contributor), Shlomo Vaknin.*
- *NLP: Psychology book for beginners! Learn communication, manipulation & inner strength - Changing consciousness, mindset & fears with Reframing - More ... and energy through Nlp (Psychology books 4) Kindle Edition by Max Krone, 24 May, 2020.*
- *NLP Workbook: A Practical Guide to Achieving the Results You Want Paperback – Import, 1 May 2021 by Joseph O'Connor.*
- *Manipulation: Techniques in Dark Psychology, Influencing People with Persuasion, NLP, and Mind Control Paperback – 22 January 2020 by Edward Benedict.*
- *NLP Expert - Explosive Techniques Of Real Neuro Linguistic Programming. How To Drastically Influence Others And How To Transform Our State Instantly, ¡In ... Dark Psychology and Manipulation Book 2) Kindle Edition by Allan Trevor, 14 Nov, 2021.*
- *The Complete Guide to Neuro-Linguistic Programming in 2019 Paperback – 3 June 2019 by Louis Sinclair.*
- *Mind Hacking: 3 Books in 1: Manipulation, How to Analyze People, NLP Paperback – Import, 20 May 2020 by Tina Berg.*
- *The Essential NLP Practitioner's Handbook: How to succeed as an NLP therapist & coach Kindle Edition by Murielle Maupoint, 30 Dec, 2017.*
- *Practical NLP: How to use NLP principles to improve your*

life and work, even if you're not NLP trained: (Book 1 in the Practical NLP series) Kindle Edition by Andy Smith, 30 April, 2013.

- *NLP: An Essential Guide: 7 (Emotional Intelligence) Paperback – Import, 29 February 2020 by Kathrin Deshotels.*
- *NLP: How To Use NLP To Persuade Others Kindle Edition by Benjamin Smith, 20Dec, 2016.*
- *NLP at Work: The Difference that Makes the Difference Revised ed. Edition, Kindle Edition by Sue Knight, 16 July,2020.*
- *Nlp: The Essential Handbook for Business: Communication Techniques to Build Relationships, Influence Others, and Achieve Your Goals Audio CD – MP3 Audio, 1 March 2021 by Jeremy Lazarus (Author), Walter Dixon (Narrator).*
- *The Power Of Thoughts & Visualization: A Deep Dive to Unlock Your Infinite Potential for Success, Happiness, Health, Abundance and Inner Peace (Inner Self Book 2) Kindle Edition by Deepak Devaraj, 24 June, 2021.*

About The Author

Dr. Amit Das, is a renowned executive advisor, consultant, educationist, author, speaker and coach whose 25+ years of business experience provides high-impact, practical solutions that support his clients' leadership development and organisational transformations. Dr. Amit Das is recognised as an innovative, principled thought leader who combines intellectual rigor and discipline with an ability to translate theory into practice. His operational skills are coupled with a strategic ability to analyse, develop, and implement successful strategies for profitability, growth, and sustainability.

Dr. Amit Das has a successful track record in aligning learning and training solutions to key business strategy with a strong focus on flawless execution excellence to facilitate individual, business divisional, and organisational performance. He keeps relentless focus on measuring training impact and ROI, people capability building graphs, training process governance, performance coaching, and strategic thinking. These have been some of his key individual success traits. His core capabilities include performance coaching, designing training and development frameworks, psychometric assessment and analysis, competency framework development and assessments, content design and facilitation of soft skills and leadership programmes, Learning Management Systems, Learning Impact Measurement, Talent Analysis, and Performance Coaching and Counselling.

He has a Ph.D. and a Fellowship in strategic learning, along with his first class degrees in Human Resource Management, Marketing Management, International Business, and Corporate Laws from the top business schools in India. He is a certified Psychometric analyst, OD

ABOUT THE AUTHOR

Interventionist, Human Psychologist, Lifecoach, Black Belt (LSS), Strategic Thinker, HR Analyst, Leadership Developer, Talent Analyst, professional Trainer from the U.K. and behavioral coach from the U.S.A.